Unlocking the Power of Digital Marketing:

A Step-by-Step Approach

Brian Ward

Contents

Chapter 1: Understanding Digital Marketing 2

Chapter 2: Building a Digital Marketing Strategy 8

Chapter 3: Search Engine Optimization (SEO) 18

Chapter 4: Content Marketing 28

Chapter 5: Social Media Marketing 37

Chapter 6: Email Marketing 47

Chapter 7: Pay-Per-Click (PPC) Advertising 57

Chapter 8: Influencer Marketing 64

Chapter 9: Content Optimization and SEO 71

Chapter 10: Analytics and Performance Measurement 81

Chapter 11: Integrated Marketing Strategies 88

Chapter 12: Future Trends in Digital Marketing 94

Chapter 13: Case Studies and Success Stories 98

Chapter 14: Digital Marketing Tools and Resources 102

Chapter 1: Understanding Digital Marketing

Introduction to Digital Marketing

Digital marketing has revolutionised the way businesses connect with their audiences. Unlike traditional marketing methods, which often rely on physical mediums such as print ads, billboards, and TV commercials, digital marketing leverages the power of the internet and electronic devices to reach consumers.

This approach allows for more targeted, measurable, and interactive marketing strategies. At its core, digital marketing encompasses all marketing efforts that use an electronic device or the internet. Businesses leverage digital channels such as search engines, social media, email, and their websites to connect with current and prospective customers.

The digital landscape is vast and continually evolving, making it crucial for marketers to stay updated on the latest trends and technologies.

The rise of smartphones, for example, has significantly influenced digital marketing strategies. Mobile-friendly websites, apps, and mobile-specific advertising campaigns are now essential components of a comprehensive digital marketing strategy.

Furthermore, the integration of artificial intelligence (AI) and machine learning into marketing tools has opened new avenues for personalised marketing and predictive analytics.

The Evolution of Digital Marketing

Digital marketing has come a long way since the inception of the internet. The first clickable banner ad, created in 1994 by AT&T, marked the beginning of the online advertising era.

This ad had a simple message: "Have you ever clicked your mouse right here? You will," and it achieved a 44% click-through rate, a figure unheard of in today's advertising landscape. This banner ad's success demonstrated the internet's potential as an advertising medium and paved the way for the development of more sophisticated digital marketing strategies.

The late 1990s and early 2000s saw the rise of search engines like Google, which became pivotal in shaping digital marketing. The introduction of Google AdWords in 2000 allowed businesses to bid for ad placement in search engine results, thus revolutionising the way companies approached advertising.

This era also witnessed the emergence of social media platforms like Facebook, Twitter, and LinkedIn, which provided new channels for brands to engage with their audiences. Today, digital marketing is an intricate and multifaceted discipline, incorporating elements such as content marketing, social media marketing, email marketing, and more.

Key Components of Digital Marketing

Digital marketing is a broad field encompassing various strategies and channels. Some of the key components include:

1. Search Engine Optimization (SEO): SEO involves optimising your website to rank higher in search engine results pages (SERPs), thereby increasing organic (non-paid) traffic to your site. This process includes on-page SEO (optimising content and HTML source code), off-page SEO (link building and social signals), and technical SEO (improving site structure and speed).
2. Content Marketing: This strategy focuses on creating and distributing valuable, relevant, and consistent content to attract and retain a clearly defined audience. The ultimate goal is to drive profitable customer action. Content marketing includes blog posts, videos, infographics, ebooks, and more.
3. Social Media Marketing: This involves promoting your brand and content on social media platforms to increase brand awareness, drive traffic, and generate leads. Popular platforms include Facebook, Instagram, Twitter, LinkedIn, and Pinterest.

4. Pay-Per-Click (PPC): PPC is a model of internet marketing in which advertisers pay a fee each time one of their ads is clicked. Essentially, it's a way of buying visits to your site rather than attempting to earn those visits organically. Google Ads is one of the most popular PPC platforms.
5. Email Marketing: This involves sending emails to prospects and customers to nurture relationships, promote products or services, and drive traffic to your website. Effective email marketing campaigns are personalised, targeted, and provide value to the recipient.
6. Affiliate Marketing: This performance-based marketing strategy involves paying a commission to external partners (affiliates) for driving traffic or sales to your business. Affiliates use their marketing channels to promote your products or services.
7. Influencer Marketing: This strategy involves partnering with influencers—individuals who have a large following and can influence their audience's purchasing decisions. Influencers promote your brand or products through their social media channels, blogs, or other platforms.
8. Online Public Relations (PR): This involves securing earned online coverage with digital publications, blogs, and other content-based websites. It's similar to traditional PR, but in the online space. Online PR includes engaging with reporters on social media, responding to comments on your website or blog, and securing positive online reviews.

The Role of Data in Digital Marketing

Data plays a crucial role in digital marketing. It allows marketers to understand their audience better, personalise their campaigns, and measure the effectiveness of their strategies. With the advent of big data and advanced analytics tools, businesses can now collect and analyse vast amounts of data from various sources, including website visits, social media interactions, email responses, and more.

For instance, tools like Google Analytics provide insights into website traffic, user behaviour, and conversion rates. Social media platforms offer analytics dashboards that track engagement metrics such as likes, shares, comments, and follower growth.

Email marketing tools like Mailchimp and Constant Contact provide data on open rates, click-through rates, and subscriber demographics. By leveraging these insights, marketers can make data-driven decisions, optimise their campaigns, and achieve better results.

Challenges in Digital Marketing

Despite its many advantages, digital marketing comes with its own set of challenges. One of the primary challenges is the ever-changing digital landscape. New technologies, platforms, and algorithms are constantly emerging, making it difficult for marketers to keep up. For example, Google frequently updates its search algorithms, which can impact website rankings and SEO strategies.

Another challenge is data privacy and security. With the increasing amount of data being collected, businesses must ensure that they comply with data protection regulations, such as the General Data Protection Regulation (GDPR) in the European Union and the California Consumer Privacy Act (CCPA) in the United States. Failure to comply with these regulations can result in hefty fines and damage to a brand's reputation.

Additionally, measuring the ROI of digital marketing efforts can be complex. While digital marketing offers numerous metrics and data points, determining which metrics are most relevant and how they translate into business success can be challenging. Marketers need to establish clear goals and KPIs (Key Performance Indicators) to effectively measure and evaluate their campaigns.

Real-World Examples of Digital Marketing Success

Several companies have successfully leveraged digital marketing to achieve remarkable results. One notable example is Coca-Cola's "Share a Coke" campaign. Launched in 2011, this campaign involved replacing the iconic Coca-Cola logo on bottles with popular names.

The campaign encouraged consumers to find bottles with their names or the names of their friends and share photos on social media using the hashtag #ShareaCoke.
This personalised approach, combined with a strong social media presence, resulted in increased sales and brand engagement.

Another example is the Dollar Shave Club. The company's founder, Michael Dubin, launched a humorous and engaging YouTube video in 2012 to promote their subscription-based razor service. The video quickly went viral, generating millions of views and significantly boosting subscriptions. The success of this video marketing campaign helped Dollar Shave Club grow rapidly and eventually led to its acquisition by Unilever for $1 billion in 2016.

Tools and Resources for Digital Marketing

There are numerous tools and resources available to help businesses with their digital marketing efforts. Some of the essential tools include:

1. Google Analytics provides insights into website traffic, user behavior, and conversion rates. Google Analytics
2. Ahrefs is an SEO tool for keyword research, backlink analysis, and competitor analysis. Ahrefs
3. Mailchimp is an email marketing platform for creating, sending, and analyzing email campaigns. Mailchimp
4. Hootsuite is a social media management tool for scheduling posts, monitoring social media activity, and analyzing performance. Hootsuite
5. Canva is a design tool for creating visual content, including social media graphics, infographics, and presentations. Canva

6. HubSpot – An all-in-one marketing platform that includes tools for CRM, email marketing, social media management, and analytics. HubSpot
7. Google Ads – A PPC advertising platform for creating and managing search ads, display ads, and video ads. Google Ads

By leveraging these tools and resources, businesses can streamline their digital marketing efforts, gain valuable insights, and achieve better results.

Conclusion

Digital marketing is a dynamic and multifaceted discipline that offers numerous opportunities for businesses to connect with their audience, drive engagement, and achieve their goals. By understanding the key components, leveraging data, and staying updated on the latest trends and technologies, marketers can create effective digital marketing strategies that deliver results. While challenges such as the ever-changing digital landscape and data privacy concerns exist, businesses that embrace digital marketing and adapt to these challenges are well-positioned for success in the digital age.

Chapter 2: Building a Digital Marketing Strategy

Introduction to Digital Marketing Strategy

A digital marketing strategy is a comprehensive plan that outlines how a business will leverage digital channels and tactics to achieve its marketing goals. It serves as a roadmap, guiding marketers in their efforts to reach, engage, and convert their target audience. A well-defined digital marketing strategy ensures that all marketing activities are aligned, consistent, and focused on achieving measurable results.

Developing an effective digital marketing strategy requires a deep understanding of the business's objectives, target audience, competitive landscape, and available resources. It involves setting clear goals, identifying the most relevant digital channels, creating compelling content, and continuously analyzing and optimizing performance.

In this chapter, we will explore the essential components of building a digital marketing strategy, including goal setting, audience research, competitive analysis, channel selection, content creation, and performance measurement.

Setting Clear Goals and Objectives

Setting clear and measurable goals is the foundation of any successful digital marketing strategy. Goals provide direction and purpose, helping marketers focus their efforts on achieving specific outcomes. When setting goals, it's important to align them with the overall business objectives and ensure they are SMART: Specific, Measurable, Achievable, Relevant, and Time-bound.

1. Specific: Goals should be clear and specific, outlining exactly what you want to achieve. For example, instead of setting a vague goal like "increase website traffic," a specific goal would be "increase website traffic by 20% over the next six months."
2. Measurable: Goals should be measurable, allowing you to track progress and determine whether you have achieved them. This involves identifying key performance indicators

(KPIs) that will help you measure success. For example, if your goal is to increase website traffic, relevant KPIs might include the number of unique visitors, page views, and sessions.

3. Achievable: Goals should be realistic and achievable, taking into account your available resources and constraints. While it's important to set ambitious goals, they should also be attainable to avoid setting your team up for failure.
4. Relevant: Goals should be relevant to your business objectives and aligned with your overall marketing strategy. For example, if your business objective is to increase sales, a relevant marketing goal might be to generate more qualified leads through your website.
5. Time-bound: Goals should have a specific timeframe for completion, providing a sense of urgency and helping you stay focused. For example, instead of setting an open-ended goal like "increase email subscribers," a time-bound goal would be "increase email subscribers by 10% within the next three months."

By setting SMART goals, you can create a clear roadmap for your digital marketing efforts and measure your progress along the way.

Conducting Audience Research

Understanding your target audience is critical to the success of your digital marketing strategy. Audience research involves gathering data and insights about your potential customers, including their demographics, behaviors, preferences, and pain points. This information helps you tailor your marketing messages and tactics to resonate with your audience and meet their needs.

1. Demographics: Demographic information includes age, gender, income, education, occupation, and location. This data helps you segment your audience and create targeted marketing campaigns. For example, if you are targeting young professionals, you might focus on social media platforms like LinkedIn and Instagram.
2. Psychographics: Psychographic information includes your audience's interests, values, attitudes, and lifestyle. Understanding psychographics helps you create content that resonates with your audience on a deeper level. For example, if your audience values sustainability, you might highlight your brand's eco-friendly practices in your marketing messages.

3. Behavioral Data: Behavioral data includes information about your audience's online activities, such as their browsing history, purchase behavior, and engagement with your content. This data helps you understand how your audience interacts with your brand and identify opportunities for improvement. For example, if you notice that users abandon their shopping carts frequently, you might implement retargeting campaigns to encourage them to complete their purchase.
4. Pain Points: Identifying your audience's pain points involves understanding the challenges and problems they face. Addressing these pain points in your marketing messages can help you position your products or services as solutions to their problems. For example, if your audience struggles with time management, you might emphasize how your product saves time and increases efficiency.

Tools for Audience Research:

- Google Analytics (https://analytics.google.com/): Provides insights into your website visitors' demographics, interests, and behaviors.
- Facebook Audience Insights (https://www.facebook.com/business/insights/tools/audience-insights): Offers detailed information about your Facebook audience, including demographics, interests, and behaviors.
- SurveyMonkey (https://www.surveymonkey.com/): A survey tool that allows you to gather feedback and insights directly from your audience.
- BuzzSumo (https://buzzsumo.com/): Helps you identify popular content and trends within your industry, providing insights into what resonates with your audience.

By conducting thorough audience research, you can create detailed buyer personas that represent different segments of your target audience. These personas serve as a reference point for your marketing efforts, ensuring that your messages and tactics are tailored to meet the needs and preferences of your potential customers.

Performing Competitive Analysis

Competitive analysis involves evaluating your competitors' strengths and weaknesses to identify opportunities and threats in the market. By understanding what your competitors are doing well and where they are falling short, you can develop strategies to differentiate your brand and gain a competitive edge.

1. Identify Your Competitors: Start by identifying your direct and indirect competitors. Direct competitors offer similar products or services to the same target audience, while indirect competitors offer alternative solutions that meet the same needs. For example, if you are a coffee shop, your direct competitors might include other local coffee shops, while your indirect competitors could include tea shops and cafes.
2. Analyze Competitor Websites: Evaluate your competitors' websites to understand their design, user experience, content, and messaging. Look for strengths and weaknesses, such as website speed, ease of navigation, and the quality of their content. Tools like SEMrush (https://www.semrush.com/) and Ahrefs (https://ahrefs.com/) can help you analyze competitors' website traffic, keywords, and backlinks.
3. Assess Social Media Presence: Analyze your competitors' social media profiles to understand their engagement strategies, content types, and posting frequency. Look at the number of followers, likes, shares, and comments to gauge their audience engagement. Tools like Hootsuite (https://hootsuite.com/) and Sprout Social (https://sproutsocial.com/) can help you monitor competitors' social media activity and performance.
4. Evaluate Content Marketing: Assess the types of content your competitors are producing, such as blog posts, videos, infographics, and ebooks. Identify the topics they cover, the quality of their content, and the level of engagement they receive. Tools like BuzzSumo (https://buzzsumo.com/) can help you identify popular content within your industry and analyze competitors' content performance.
5. Analyze SEO Strategy: Evaluate your competitors' SEO strategies by analyzing their keyword rankings, backlink profiles, and on-page optimization. Tools like Moz (https://moz.com/) and SEMrush (https://www.semrush.com/) can help you identify the keywords your competitors are targeting and their backlink sources.

6. **Assess Paid Advertising:** Analyze your competitors' paid advertising campaigns, including search ads, display ads, and social media ads. Look at the ad copy, design, targeting, and call-to-action to understand their strategies. Tools like SpyFu (https://www.spyfu.com/) and AdEspresso (https://adespresso.com/) can help you monitor competitors' PPC campaigns and ad performance.

By performing a comprehensive competitive analysis, you can identify gaps and opportunities in the market, refine your value proposition, and develop strategies to differentiate your brand. Understanding your competitors' strengths and weaknesses allows you to capitalize on their shortcomings and build a competitive advantage.

Selecting Digital Marketing Channels

Selecting the right digital marketing channels is crucial for reaching and engaging your target audience. Different channels offer unique advantages and serve different purposes, so it's important to choose the ones that align with your goals and audience preferences.

1. **Search Engine Optimization (SEO):** SEO is essential for driving organic traffic to your website. By optimizing your website for search engines, you can increase your visibility in search results and attract visitors who are actively searching for your products or services. Key SEO strategies include keyword research, on-page optimization, technical SEO, and link building.
2. **Content Marketing:** Content marketing involves creating and distributing valuable content to attract and engage your audience. This can include blog posts, videos, infographics, ebooks, and more. Content marketing helps establish your brand as an authority, build trust with your audience, and drive traffic to your website.
3. **Social Media Marketing:** Social media platforms like Facebook, Instagram, Twitter, LinkedIn, and Pinterest offer opportunities to connect with your audience, build brand awareness, and drive engagement. Each platform has its own unique features and user base, so it's important to choose the ones that align with your target audience and marketing goals.
4. **Pay-Per-Click (PPC) Advertising:** PPC advertising allows you to display ads on search engines, social media platforms, and other websites. You pay a fee each time someone

clicks on your ad. PPC is an effective way to drive immediate traffic and generate leads, especially for time-sensitive promotions and competitive keywords. Popular PPC platforms include Google Ads and Facebook Ads.

5. Email Marketing: Email marketing involves sending personalized and targeted emails to your subscribers. It is an effective way to nurture relationships, promote products or services, and drive conversions. Key email marketing strategies include segmentation, automation, and A/B testing.

6. Influencer Marketing: Influencer marketing involves partnering with influencers who have a large following and can influence their audience's purchasing decisions. Influencers promote your brand or products through their social media channels, blogs, or other platforms. This strategy can help you reach a wider audience and build credibility.

7. Affiliate Marketing: Affiliate marketing is a performance-based strategy where you pay a commission to external partners (affiliates) for driving traffic or sales to your business. Affiliates use their marketing channels to promote your products or services, and you only pay them when they deliver results.

8. Online Public Relations (PR): Online PR involves securing earned online coverage with digital publications, blogs, and other content-based websites. This can include press releases, media relations, influencer outreach, and securing positive reviews. Effective online PR helps build brand credibility, enhance visibility, and drive traffic to your website.

Creating Compelling Content

Content is the backbone of digital marketing. High-quality, relevant, and engaging content attracts and retains your audience, encourages interaction, and drives conversions. To create compelling content, you need to focus on understanding your audience, delivering value, and maintaining consistency.

1. Understanding Your Audience: Knowing your audience's preferences, interests, and pain points is crucial for creating content that resonates with them. Use audience research and buyer personas to gain insights into what your audience cares about and tailor your content to meet their needs.
2. Delivering Value: Your content should provide value to your audience, whether it's through educating, entertaining, or inspiring them. Answer common questions, solve problems, and offer insights that your audience can't find elsewhere. Valuable content builds trust and positions your brand as an authority in your industry.
3. Maintaining Consistency: Consistent content creation and publishing are key to keeping your audience engaged and coming back for more. Develop a content calendar that outlines your content topics, formats, and publishing schedule. Stick to the schedule to ensure a steady flow of content.

Types of Content:

- Blog Posts: In-depth articles that provide valuable information, insights, and solutions to your audience's problems. Blog posts help improve SEO, drive organic traffic, and establish your brand as an authority.
- Videos: Engaging and dynamic content that captures attention and conveys information effectively. Videos can be used for tutorials, product demos, interviews, and behind-the-scenes looks.
- Infographics: Visual content that presents data and information in an easily digestible format. Infographics are highly shareable and can help simplify complex topics.
- Ebooks and Whitepapers: Comprehensive guides that provide in-depth knowledge on specific topics. These can be used as lead magnets to capture email addresses and generate leads.
- Case Studies: Detailed accounts of how your products or services have helped customers achieve their goals. Case studies provide social proof and demonstrate the value of your offerings.
- Social Media Posts: Short and engaging content tailored for social media platforms. These can include images, videos, polls, and user-generated content.

- Podcasts: Audio content that allows you to share insights, interviews, and discussions with your audience. Podcasts are convenient for on-the-go consumption.

Tools for Content Creation:

- Canva (https://www.canva.com/): A design tool for creating visually appealing graphics, infographics, and social media posts.
- Adobe Creative Cloud (https://www.adobe.com/creativecloud.html): A suite of professional design tools, including Photoshop, Illustrator, and Premiere Pro, for creating high-quality visual and video content.
- Grammarly (https://www.grammarly.com/): A writing assistant that helps you produce clear, error-free, and engaging written content.
- Lumen5 (https://www.lumen5.com/): A video creation platform that turns blog posts and articles into engaging videos.

Measuring and Analyzing Performance

Measuring and analyzing the performance of your digital marketing efforts is crucial for understanding what works, what doesn't, and how you can improve. By tracking key metrics and analyzing data, you can make data-driven decisions and optimize your strategy for better results.

1. Website Analytics: Website analytics tools like Google Analytics provide insights into your website traffic, user behavior, and conversion rates. Key metrics to track include the number of unique visitors, page views, bounce rate, average session duration, and conversion rate. These metrics help you understand how users interact with your website and identify areas for improvement.
2. Social Media Analytics: Social media platforms offer analytics dashboards that track engagement metrics such as likes, shares, comments, and follower growth. Tools like Hootsuite and Sprout Social provide detailed social media analytics and reporting features. Key metrics to track include reach, engagement rate, click-through rate (CTR), and follower growth.
3. Email Marketing Analytics: Email marketing tools like Mailchimp and Constant Contact provide data on open rates, click-through rates, and subscriber demographics. Key metrics to track include open rate, CTR, bounce rate, and unsubscribe rate. These metrics

help you evaluate the effectiveness of your email campaigns and identify opportunities for optimization.
4. PPC Advertising Analytics: PPC platforms like Google Ads and Facebook Ads offer analytics dashboards that track ad performance metrics such as impressions, clicks, CTR, cost-per-click (CPC), and conversion rate. These metrics help you evaluate the effectiveness of your paid advertising campaigns and optimize your bidding and targeting strategies.
5. SEO Analytics: SEO tools like Ahrefs and Moz provide insights into your keyword rankings, backlink profile, and organic traffic. Key metrics to track include organic traffic, keyword rankings, domain authority, and backlink quality. These metrics help you evaluate the effectiveness of your SEO efforts and identify opportunities for improvement.

Tools for Measuring and Analyzing Performance:

- Google Analytics (https://analytics.google.com/): Provides insights into website traffic, user behavior, and conversion rates.
- Hootsuite (https://hootsuite.com/): A social media management tool with robust analytics and reporting features.
- Mailchimp (https://mailchimp.com/): An email marketing platform with detailed analytics and reporting features.
- Google Data Studio (https://datastudio.google.com/): A data visualization tool that allows you to create customizable and interactive reports and dashboards.
- Ahrefs (https://ahrefs.com/): An SEO tool for tracking keyword performance, backlinks, and organic traffic.

By regularly measuring and analyzing the performance of your digital marketing efforts, you can gain valuable insights into what's working, what's not, and how you can improve. Use these insights to make data-driven decisions, optimize your strategy, and achieve better results.

Conclusion

Building a digital marketing strategy is a comprehensive process that involves setting clear goals, conducting audience research, performing competitive analysis, selecting the right channels, creating compelling content, and measuring performance. By following these steps and leveraging the right tools, businesses can develop effective digital marketing strategies that drive engagement, conversions, and growth. Regularly review and refine your strategy to stay ahead of trends, adapt to changes, and continuously improve your marketing efforts.

Chapter 3: Search Engine Optimization (SEO)

Introduction to SEO

Search Engine Optimization (SEO) is the practice of optimizing your website to rank higher in search engine results pages (SERPs). The primary goal of SEO is to increase organic (non-paid) traffic to your website by improving its visibility for relevant search queries. SEO involves a combination of on-page, off-page, and technical optimization techniques to enhance your website's relevance, authority, and user experience.

SEO is a dynamic and ever-evolving field, influenced by changes in search engine algorithms, user behavior, and technological advancements. To succeed in SEO, marketers must stay updated on the latest trends, best practices, and algorithm updates. In this chapter, we will explore the key components of SEO, including keyword research, on-page optimization, technical SEO, content creation, and link building.

The Importance of SEO

SEO is crucial for several reasons:

1. Increased Visibility: Higher rankings in search engine results pages lead to increased visibility and exposure to potential customers. Most users tend to click on the top results, so ranking higher can significantly boost your website traffic.
2. Organic Traffic: Organic traffic is the most valuable type of traffic because it is highly targeted and cost-effective. Unlike paid advertising, organic traffic doesn't require ongoing payments, making it a sustainable, long-term strategy.
3. Credibility and Trust: Websites that rank higher in search results are often perceived as more credible and trustworthy by users. Achieving high rankings can enhance your brand's reputation and authority in your industry.
4. User Experience: SEO involves optimizing your website's structure, speed, and usability, which improves the overall user experience. A well-optimized website is easier to navigate, loads quickly, and provides valuable content, leading to higher user satisfaction.

5. Competitive Advantage: SEO provides a competitive advantage by helping you outrank competitors and capture a larger share of organic traffic. A strong SEO strategy can differentiate your brand and position you as a leader in your industry.

Keyword Research

Keyword research is the foundation of SEO. It involves identifying the search terms and phrases that users enter into search engines when looking for information, products, or services related to your business. By targeting the right keywords, you can attract relevant traffic to your website and improve your chances of ranking higher in search results.

1. Identifying Relevant Keywords: Start by brainstorming a list of topics and terms related to your business. Think about the words and phrases your target audience might use when searching for your products or services. Use tools like Google Keyword Planner (https://ads.google.com/home/tools/keyword-planner/), Ahrefs (https://ahrefs.com/), and SEMrush (https://www.semrush.com/) to generate keyword ideas and identify search volume, competition, and keyword difficulty.

2. Long-Tail Keywords: Long-tail keywords are longer, more specific phrases that typically have lower search volume but higher conversion potential. While short-tail keywords (e.g., "shoes") are highly competitive, long-tail keywords (e.g., "best running shoes for flat feet") are less competitive and more targeted. Incorporating long-tail keywords into your SEO strategy can help you attract highly relevant traffic and improve your chances of ranking.

3. Analyzing Competitor Keywords: Analyzing your competitors' keywords can provide valuable insights into their SEO strategies and help you identify opportunities. Use tools like Ahrefs (https://ahrefs.com/), SEMrush (https://www.semrush.com/), and SpyFu (https://www.spyfu.com/) to discover the keywords your competitors are ranking for, their search volumes, and their backlink profiles. This information can help you refine your keyword strategy and target keywords that your competitors may have overlooked.

4. Keyword Intent: Understanding the intent behind a keyword is crucial for creating content that meets user expectations. There are four main types of keyword intent: informational (e.g., "how to fix a leaky faucet"), navigational (e.g., "Facebook login"), transactional (e.g., "buy running shoes"), and commercial investigation (e.g., "best

running shoes 2024"). By aligning your content with the user's intent, you can improve user engagement and increase the likelihood of ranking higher in search results.

On-Page Optimization

On-page optimization involves optimizing individual pages on your website to rank higher in search results and attract relevant traffic. This includes optimizing content, HTML source code, and overall user experience. Key elements of on-page optimization include:

1. Title Tags: The title tag is an HTML element that specifies the title of a web page. It is displayed on search engine results pages (SERPs) as the clickable headline. Title tags should be unique, descriptive, and include the target keyword. Keep the title length between 50-60 characters to ensure it displays properly in search results.
2. Meta Descriptions: The meta description is an HTML element that provides a brief summary of a web page. It appears below the title tag in search results and can influence click-through rates. Meta descriptions should be compelling, informative, and include the target keyword. Keep the description length between 150-160 characters.
3. Header Tags (H1, H2, H3, etc.): Header tags help structure your content and make it easier for search engines and users to understand the hierarchy of information. The H1 tag should include the primary keyword and serve as the main heading of the page. Use H2, H3, and other header tags to break down content into logical sections and sub-sections.
4. URL Structure: URLs should be short, descriptive, and include the target keyword. Avoid using special characters, numbers, and unnecessary words. Clean and user-friendly URLs improve click-through rates and make it easier for search engines to crawl and index your pages.
5. Content Optimization: High-quality, relevant, and engaging content is crucial for SEO. Ensure that your content provides value to users, addresses their needs, and answers their questions. Use the target keyword naturally throughout the content, including in the introduction, body, and conclusion. Avoid keyword stuffing, as it can harm your rankings.
6. Internal Linking: Internal links connect different pages on your website and help search engines understand the structure and hierarchy of your content. They also improve user

experience by guiding visitors to relevant pages. Use descriptive anchor text and link to relevant pages to enhance your internal linking strategy.

7. Image Optimization: Images enhance the visual appeal of your content and improve user engagement. Optimize images by using descriptive file names, adding alt text, and compressing file sizes to improve loading times. Alt text should describe the image and include the target keyword when relevant.

Tools for On-Page Optimization:

- Yoast SEO (https://yoast.com/): A WordPress plugin that helps optimize your content for search engines by providing real-time feedback and recommendations.
- Moz On-Page Grader (https://moz.com/products/pro/on-page-grader): Analyzes your web pages and provides actionable insights to improve on-page optimization.
- Screaming Frog (https://www.screamingfrog.co.uk/seo-spider/): A website crawler that helps identify on-page SEO issues, such as broken links, duplicate content, and missing meta tags.

Technical SEO

Technical SEO involves optimizing the technical aspects of your website to improve its crawlability, indexability, and overall performance. Key elements of technical SEO include:

1. Website Speed: Page load speed is a critical ranking factor and directly impacts user experience. Slow-loading pages can lead to higher bounce rates and lower rankings. Optimize your website's speed by compressing images, minifying CSS and JavaScript files, leveraging browser caching, and using a content delivery network (CDN).
2. Mobile-Friendliness: With the increasing use of mobile devices, having a mobile-friendly website is essential for SEO. Ensure that your website is responsive and provides a seamless experience across all devices. Use Google's Mobile-Friendly Test (https://search.google.com/test/mobile-friendly) to check your website's mobile compatibility.
3. XML Sitemap: An XML sitemap is a file that lists all the important pages on your website and helps search engines crawl and index your content. Submit your XML sitemap to Google Search Console (https://search.google.com/search-console/) and Bing

Webmaster Tools (https://www.bing.com/toolbox/webmaster) to ensure that search engines can discover and index your pages.
4. Robots.txt: The robots.txt file is used to control which pages search engines can and cannot crawl. Ensure that your robots.txt file is correctly configured and does not block important pages from being indexed.
5. Secure Websites (HTTPS): Secure websites (HTTPS) are preferred by search engines and users. Install an SSL certificate to encrypt data and ensure that your website is secure. Google considers HTTPS as a ranking signal, so having a secure website can positively impact your rankings.
6. Structured Data and Schema Markup: Structured data and schema markup help search engines understand the content and context of your web pages. Implementing schema markup can enhance your search results with rich snippets, such as star ratings, reviews, and event details. Use Google's Structured Data Markup Helper (https://www.google.com/webmasters/markup-helper/) to generate and test schema markup for your website.

Tools for Technical SEO:

- Google PageSpeed Insights (https://developers.google.com/speed/pagespeed/insights/): Analyzes your website's speed and provides recommendations for improvement.
- GTmetrix (https://gtmetrix.com/): A website performance testing tool that provides insights and recommendations for improving loading times.
- Screaming Frog (https://www.screamingfrog.co.uk/seo-spider/): A website crawler that helps identify technical SEO issues, such as broken links, duplicate content, and missing meta tags.
- Google Search Console (https://search.google.com/search-console/): Provides insights into your website's performance, crawl errors, and indexing status.

Content Creation for SEO

Creating high-quality, relevant, and engaging content is essential for SEO. Content that provides value to users and addresses their needs is more likely to rank higher in search results. Key elements of content creation for SEO include:

1. Keyword Integration: Incorporate the target keyword naturally throughout the content, including in the title, headers, introduction, body, and conclusion. Avoid keyword stuffing, as it can harm your rankings and negatively impact user experience.
2. Content Length and Depth: Longer, in-depth content tends to perform better in search results. Aim to create comprehensive content that covers the topic thoroughly and provides valuable insights. However, prioritize quality over quantity, and ensure that the content remains engaging and easy to read.
3. Readability and Structure: Write content that is easy to read and understand. Use short paragraphs, bullet points, and subheadings to break up the text and improve readability. Use a conversational tone and avoid jargon or complex language.
4. Visual Content: Incorporate visual elements like images, infographics, videos, and charts to enhance the content and improve user engagement. Visual content can help illustrate key points, simplify complex topics, and make the content more appealing.
5. Internal and External Links: Include internal links to relevant pages on your website to improve navigation and guide users to additional content. Use external links to reputable sources to provide additional context and support your points.
6. Regular Updates: Regularly update your content to ensure that it remains accurate, relevant, and up-to-date. Search engines favor fresh content, and updating your articles can help maintain or improve their rankings.

Tools for Content Creation:

- Grammarly (https://www.grammarly.com/): A writing assistant that helps you produce clear, error-free, and engaging written content.
- Hemingway Editor (http://www.hemingwayapp.com/): A writing tool that improves readability by identifying complex sentences and suggesting simpler alternatives.
- Canva (https://www.canva.com/): A design tool for creating visually appealing graphics, infographics, and social media posts.
- BuzzSumo (https://buzzsumo.com/): Helps you identify popular content and trends within your industry, providing insights into what resonates with your audience.

Link Building

Link building is the process of acquiring high-quality backlinks from other websites to improve your website's authority and rankings. Backlinks are a key ranking factor, and search engines view them as endorsements of your content. Effective link building involves:

1. Creating Link-Worthy Content: High-quality, valuable, and shareable content is more likely to attract backlinks. Create content that addresses common questions, solves problems, or provides unique insights. Examples of link-worthy content include in-depth guides, original research, infographics, and case studies.
2. Guest Blogging: Contributing guest posts to reputable websites in your industry can help you earn backlinks and expand your reach. When guest blogging, focus on providing valuable content and include a link back to your website in your author bio or within the content (if allowed). Reach out to websites that accept guest posts and pitch topics that are relevant to their audience.
3. Building Relationships: Establish relationships with influencers, bloggers, and industry experts. Networking can lead to natural backlink opportunities as these individuals may reference or share your content. Engage with them on social media, attend industry events, and participate in relevant online communities.
4. Broken Link Building: Identify broken links on other websites and suggest your content as a replacement. Use tools like Ahrefs (https://ahrefs.com/) or Check My Links (https://chrome.google.com/webstore/detail/check-my-links/ojkcdipcgfaekbeaelaapakgnjflfglf) to find broken links on relevant websites. Reach out to the website owner or editor and offer your content as a solution.
5. Skyscraper Technique: The skyscraper technique involves finding high-performing content in your industry, creating a better version, and reaching out to websites that link to the original content. Use tools like BuzzSumo (https://buzzsumo.com/) to identify popular content and analyze its backlinks. Create content that is more comprehensive, up-to-date, and valuable, then reach out to the linking websites and suggest your improved version.
6. Resource Pages: Many websites have resource or link pages that list valuable content related to a specific topic. Find resource pages in your industry and reach out to the

website owners, suggesting your content as a valuable addition. Use search queries like "keyword + resource page" or "keyword + inurl:links" to find relevant pages.

7. Content Promotion: Actively promote your content through social media, email newsletters, and online communities to increase its visibility and attract backlinks. The more people see and engage with your content, the higher the chances of earning backlinks.

Tools for Link Building:

- Ahrefs (https://ahrefs.com/): A comprehensive SEO tool that helps you analyze backlinks, identify link opportunities, and track your link-building efforts.
- Moz Link Explorer (https://moz.com/link-explorer): A backlink analysis tool that provides insights into your website's link profile and helps you find link-building opportunities.
- BuzzStream (https://www.buzzstream.com/): A link-building and outreach tool that helps you manage relationships, track emails, and monitor link-building campaigns.
- Hunter (https://hunter.io/): A tool that helps you find email addresses for outreach and link-building purposes.

Measuring SEO Performance

Measuring the performance of your SEO efforts is essential for understanding what's working, what's not, and how you can improve. By tracking key metrics and analyzing the data, you can make data-driven decisions and optimize your SEO strategy for better results. Key metrics to track include:

1. Organic Traffic: The number of visitors who arrive at your website through organic search results. Tools like Google Analytics (https://analytics.google.com/) provide detailed insights into your organic traffic, including the sources, user behavior, and conversion rates.
2. Keyword Rankings: The positions of your target keywords in search engine results pages (SERPs). Use tools like Ahrefs (https://ahrefs.com/), SEMrush (https://www.semrush.com/), and Moz (https://moz.com/) to track your keyword rankings and monitor changes over time.

3. Backlinks: The number and quality of backlinks pointing to your website. Tools like Ahrefs (https://ahrefs.com/), Moz Link Explorer (https://moz.com/link-explorer), and Majestic (https://majestic.com/) help you analyze your backlink profile and identify link-building opportunities.
4. Click-Through Rate (CTR): The percentage of users who click on your search engine listing when it appears in search results. Higher CTRs indicate that your title tags and meta descriptions are compelling and relevant. Use Google Search Console (https://search.google.com/search-console/) to monitor your CTR and identify opportunities for improvement.
5. Bounce Rate: The percentage of visitors who leave your website after viewing only one page. A high bounce rate may indicate that your content or user experience needs improvement. Use Google Analytics (https://analytics.google.com/) to track your bounce rate and identify pages with high exit rates.
6. Conversion Rate: The percentage of visitors who complete a desired action, such as making a purchase, filling out a form, or signing up for a newsletter. Conversion rate is a key indicator of the effectiveness of your SEO efforts in driving valuable actions. Use Google Analytics (https://analytics.google.com/) to track your conversion rates and set up goals.
7. Page Load Time: The time it takes for your web pages to load. Page load time is a critical ranking factor and directly impacts user experience. Use tools like Google PageSpeed Insights (https://developers.google.com/speed/pagespeed/insights/) and GTmetrix (https://gtmetrix.com/) to measure and optimize your page load times.

Tools for Measuring SEO Performance:

- Google Analytics (https://analytics.google.com/): Provides insights into website traffic, user behavior, and conversion rates.
- Google Search Console (https://search.google.com/search-console/): Offers data on your website's performance in search results, including keyword rankings, CTR, and crawl errors.
- Ahrefs (https://ahrefs.com/): A comprehensive SEO tool for tracking keyword rankings, backlinks, and organic traffic.

- SEMrush (https://www.semrush.com/) is anAn all-in-one SEO tool for keyword research, competitor analysis, and performance tracking.
- Moz (https://moz.com/): Provides tools for keyword tracking, backlink analysis, and on-page optimization.

By regularly measuring and analyzing the performance of your SEO efforts, you can gain valuable insights into what's working, what's not, and how you can improve. Use these insights to make data-driven decisions, optimize your strategy, and achieve better results.

Conclusion

Search Engine Optimization (SEO) is a dynamic and multifaceted discipline that plays a crucial role in driving organic traffic, enhancing visibility, and building credibility. By mastering the key components of SEO—keyword research, on-page optimization, technical SEO, content creation, and link building—businesses can improve their search rankings and achieve sustainable growth. Regularly measuring and analyzing performance is essential for making data-driven decisions and continuously optimizing your SEO strategy. Stay updated on the latest trends, algorithm updates, and best practices to remain competitive in the ever-evolving landscape of SEO.

Chapter 4: Content Marketing

Introduction to Content Marketing

Content marketing is a strategic approach focused on creating and distributing valuable, relevant, and consistent content to attract and engage a clearly defined audience. The ultimate goal of content marketing is to drive profitable customer action, whether it's generating leads, increasing sales, or building brand loyalty. Unlike traditional marketing, which often involves direct promotion, content marketing aims to provide value to the audience and build trust over time.

In the digital age, content marketing has become a cornerstone of successful marketing strategies. With the proliferation of online channels and the increasing demand for valuable information, businesses must prioritize content creation to stay competitive. This chapter will explore the key components of content marketing, including content strategy, content creation, distribution, and measurement.

The Importance of Content Marketing

Content marketing is crucial for several reasons:

Builds Trust and Credibility: High-quality content establishes your brand as an authority and builds trust with your audience. By consistently providing valuable information, you can position your brand as a reliable source of knowledge in your industry.

1. Drives Organic Traffic: Well-optimized content can improve your search engine rankings and drive organic traffic to your website. Content marketing and SEO go hand in hand, as valuable content attracts backlinks, increases dwell time, and signals relevance to search engines.

2. Engages and Educates: Content marketing provides valuable information that engages and educates your audience, helping them make informed decisions. Educational content, such as how-to guides, tutorials, and industry insights, can address your audience's pain points and provide solutions.

3. Generates Leads: Content can attract potential customers and nurture them through the sales funnel, generating leads and driving conversions. Lead magnets, such as ebooks,

webinars, and whitepapers, can capture email addresses and initiate the lead nurturing process.
4. Supports Other Marketing Efforts: Content marketing complements and enhances other marketing strategies, such as social media, email marketing, and PPC advertising. Compelling content can be repurposed and distributed across various channels to maximize its impact.

Developing a Content Strategy

A content strategy is a comprehensive plan that outlines how you will create, distribute, and manage content to achieve your marketing goals. Developing a content strategy involves several key steps:

1. Define Your Goals: Clearly define the goals of your content marketing strategy. Are you looking to increase brand awareness, drive traffic, generate leads, or educate your audience? Your goals will guide your content planning and creation. For example, if your goal is to generate leads, you might focus on creating lead magnets, such as ebooks and webinars, to capture email addresses.
2. Understand Your Audience: Conduct audience research to understand your target audience's needs, preferences, and pain points. Create buyer personas to represent different segments of your audience and tailor your content to their interests. For example, if your audience consists of small business owners, you might create content that addresses their challenges, such as cash flow management and marketing strategies.
3. Conduct a Content Audit: Perform a content audit to assess your existing content and identify gaps, strengths, and areas for improvement. Analyze the performance of your current content to understand what resonates with your audience. Use tools like Google Analytics (https://analytics.google.com/) and SEMrush (https://www.semrush.com/) to evaluate metrics such as page views, engagement, bounce rates, and conversion rates. Identify high-performing content that you can repurpose or update, and note areas where new content is needed to fill gaps.
4. Develop a Content Plan: Create a content plan that outlines the types of content you will produce, the topics you will cover, the formats you will use, and the publishing schedule. Your content plan should align with your marketing goals and audience preferences. For

example, if your target audience prefers visual content, you might prioritize creating videos and infographics.

5. Content Creation and Optimization: Focus on creating high-quality, valuable, and engaging content that addresses your audience's needs and aligns with your goals. Incorporate SEO best practices, such as keyword integration, internal linking, and optimization of title tags and meta descriptions, to improve your content's visibility in search results.

6. Distribution and Promotion: Develop a distribution strategy to ensure your content reaches your target audience. Leverage multiple channels, including your website, social media, email marketing, and third-party platforms. Promote your content through organic and paid methods to maximize its reach and impact.

7. Measure and Analyze Performance: Continuously measure and analyze the performance of your content to understand what works, what doesn't, and how you can improve. Use analytics tools to track key metrics, such as traffic, engagement, leads, and conversions. Use these insights to refine your content strategy and optimize your efforts for better results.

Tools for Content Strategy:

- Trello (https://trello.com/): A project management tool that helps you organize and manage your content plan and publishing schedule.
- CoSchedule (https://coschedule.com/): A content marketing platform that provides tools for planning, scheduling, and distributing content.
- Google Analytics (https://analytics.google.com/): Provides insights into your content performance, including traffic, engagement, and conversion metrics.
- SEMrush (https://www.semrush.com/): An all-in-one marketing tool that offers content audit, keyword research, and performance tracking features.

Content Creation

Content creation is the process of generating ideas, producing content, and making it available to your audience. Effective content creation involves understanding your audience, delivering value, and maintaining consistency.

1. Understanding Your Audience: Knowing your audience's preferences, interests, and pain points is crucial for creating content that resonates with them. Use audience research and buyer personas to gain insights into what your audience cares about and tailor your content to meet their needs.
2. Delivering Value: Your content should provide value to your audience, whether it's through educating, entertaining, or inspiring them. Answer common questions, solve problems, and offer insights that your audience can't find elsewhere. Valuable content builds trust and positions your brand as an authority in your industry.
3. Maintaining Consistency: Consistent content creation and publishing are key to keeping your audience engaged and coming back for more. Develop a content calendar that outlines your content topics, formats, and publishing schedule. Stick to the schedule to ensure a steady flow of content.

Types of Content:

- Blog Posts: In-depth articles that provide valuable information, insights, and solutions to your audience's problems. Blog posts help improve SEO, drive organic traffic, and establish your brand as an authority.
- Videos: Engaging and dynamic content that captures attention and conveys information effectively. Videos can be used for tutorials, product demos, interviews, and behind-the-scenes looks.
- Infographics: Visual content that presents data and information in an easily digestible format. Infographics are highly shareable and can help simplify complex topics.

- Ebooks and Whitepapers: Comprehensive guides that provide in-depth knowledge on specific topics. These can be used as lead magnets to capture email addresses and generate leads.
- Case Studies: Detailed accounts of how your products or services have helped customers achieve their goals. Case studies provide social proof and demonstrate the value of your offerings.
- Social Media Posts: Short and engaging content tailored for social media platforms. These can include images, videos, polls, and user-generated content.
- Podcasts: Audio content that allows you to share insights, interviews, and discussions with your audience. Podcasts are convenient for on-the-go consumption.

Tools for Content Creation:

- Canva (https://www.canva.com/): A design tool for creating visually appealing graphics, infographics, and social media posts.
- Adobe Creative Cloud (https://www.adobe.com/creativecloud.html): A suite of professional design tools, including Photoshop, Illustrator, and Premiere Pro, for creating high-quality visual and video content.
- Grammarly (https://www.grammarly.com/): A writing assistant that helps you produce clear, error-free, and engaging written content.
- Lumen5 (https://www.lumen5.com/): A video creation platform that turns blog posts and articles into engaging videos.

Content Distribution and Promotion

Creating valuable content is just one part of the equation; you also need to ensure that your content reaches your target audience. Content distribution and promotion involve sharing your content across various channels to maximize its visibility and impact.

1. Owned Media: Owned media refers to the channels that you control, such as your website, blog, email newsletter, and social media profiles. Regularly publish content on your owned media channels and promote it to your existing audience. For example, share your latest blog post on your social media profiles and include it in your email newsletter.

2. Earned Media: Earned media refers to the coverage and exposure you receive from third-party sources, such as media outlets, influencers, and user-generated content. Earned media is typically generated through PR efforts, influencer outreach, and content that naturally attracts attention and shares. For example, if a popular industry blog features your content, it can drive significant traffic and credibility to your website.
3. Paid Media: Paid media involves promoting your content through paid channels, such as search engine advertising, social media ads, and sponsored content. Paid media can help you reach a wider audience and drive immediate traffic to your content. For example, you can use Facebook Ads to promote a valuable ebook and capture leads.

Content Distribution Channels:

- Social Media: Share your content on platforms like Facebook, Twitter, LinkedIn, Instagram, and Pinterest to reach and engage your audience. Tailor your content to fit the unique features and audience preferences of each platform.
- Email Marketing: Use email newsletters to distribute your content to your subscribers. Personalize your emails and segment your audience to deliver relevant content that resonates with each segment.
- Content Syndication: Syndicate your content on third-party platforms, such as Medium, LinkedIn Pulse, and industry-specific websites, to reach a broader audience. Ensure that you follow best practices for syndication to avoid duplicate content issues.
- Influencer Partnerships: Collaborate with influencers and industry experts to promote your content. Influencers can help you reach their followers and build credibility in your niche.
- PR and Media Outreach: Pitch your content to media outlets, bloggers, and journalists who cover topics related to your industry. Secure media coverage to increase your content's visibility and credibility.

Tools for Content Distribution and Promotion:

- Buffer (https://buffer.com/): A social media scheduling tool that helps you plan and promote your content across multiple platforms.
- Mailchimp (https://mailchimp.com/): An email marketing platform for creating and sending newsletters that feature your content.

- Outbrain (https://www.outbrain.com/): A content discovery platform that promotes your content on high-traffic websites.
- BuzzSumo (https://buzzsumo.com/): Helps you identify influencers and popular content within your industry for outreach and promotion.

Measuring Content Marketing Performance

Measuring the performance of your content marketing efforts is essential for understanding what's working, what's not, and how you can improve. By tracking key metrics and analyzing data, you can make data-driven decisions and optimize your content strategy for better results.

1. Traffic Metrics: Measure the amount of traffic your content generates, including unique visitors, page views, and sessions. Tools like Google Analytics (https://analytics.google.com/) provide detailed insights into your traffic sources, user behavior, and engagement metrics.
2. Engagement Metrics: Track how users interact with your content, including time on page, bounce rate, social shares, and comments. High engagement indicates that your content resonates with your audience and provides value.
3. Lead Generation Metrics: Measure the number of leads generated through your content, such as email sign-ups, form submissions, and downloads. Track the performance of lead magnets, such as ebooks, webinars, and whitepapers, to understand their impact on lead generation.
4. Conversion Metrics: Track the number of conversions generated through your content, such as purchases, sign-ups, or other desired actions. Use tools like Google Analytics (https://analytics.google.com/) to set up goals and track conversion rates.
5. SEO Metrics: Monitor your content's performance in search engine rankings, including keyword rankings, organic traffic, and backlinks. Tools like Ahrefs (https://ahrefs.com/), SEMrush (https://www.semrush.com/), and Moz (https://moz.com/) provide insights into your content's SEO performance.
6. ROI Metrics: Calculate the return on investment (ROI) of your content marketing efforts by comparing the revenue generated to the costs incurred. ROI helps you determine the financial effectiveness of your content strategy and allocate resources accordingly.

Tools for Measuring Content Marketing Performance:

- Google Analytics (https://analytics.google.com/): Provides insights into website traffic, user behavior, and conversion rates.
- HubSpot (https://www.hubspot.com/): An all-in-one marketing platform that includes tools for content performance tracking, lead generation, and ROI measurement.
- BuzzSumo (https://buzzsumo.com/): Helps you track social shares and engagement metrics for your content.
- SEMrush (https://www.semrush.com/): An all-in-one SEO tool that offers keyword tracking, backlink analysis, and content performance insights.

By regularly measuring and analyzing the performance of your content marketing efforts, you can gain valuable insights into what resonates with your audience and drives desired actions. Use these insights to refine your content strategy, optimize your efforts, and achieve better results.

Real-World Examples of Successful Content Marketing

Several companies have successfully leveraged content marketing to achieve remarkable results. Here are a few notable examples:

1. HubSpot: HubSpot is a leading provider of inbound marketing and sales software. The company has built a reputation for producing high-quality, informative content that educates and empowers marketers and sales professionals. HubSpot's blog covers a wide range of topics, including marketing, sales, customer service, and productivity. The company also offers valuable resources such as ebooks, webinars, and templates. HubSpot's content marketing efforts have played a significant role in driving traffic, generating leads, and establishing the brand as an industry authority.

2. Buffer: Buffer is a social media management tool that has gained widespread recognition through its content marketing strategy. Buffer's blog focuses on social media marketing, productivity, and remote work, providing valuable insights and actionable tips. The company also publishes in-depth case studies, research reports, and guest posts from industry experts. Buffer's transparent approach, including sharing the company's growth and revenue numbers, has contributed to building trust and credibility with its audience.
3. GoPro: GoPro, a manufacturer of action cameras, has effectively used user-generated content (UGC) to promote its products. The company encourages customers to share their GoPro-captured adventures and experiences on social media using the hashtag #GoPro. GoPro features the best UGC on its website, social media profiles, and YouTube channel, showcasing the versatility and quality of its cameras. This strategy has helped GoPro build a strong community of loyal customers and generate authentic, engaging content that resonates with its audience.
4. Moz: Moz, a provider of SEO software and tools, has built a reputation for producing valuable, educational content for the SEO and digital marketing community. Moz's blog covers a wide range of SEO topics, including keyword research, link building, technical SEO, and content marketing. The company also offers resources such as the Beginner's Guide to SEO, Whiteboard Friday videos, and in-depth research reports. Moz's commitment to providing high-quality content has established the brand as a trusted authority in the SEO industry.

Conclusion

Content marketing is a powerful strategy for attracting, engaging, and converting your target audience. By developing a comprehensive content strategy, creating high-quality and valuable content, distributing and promoting your content effectively, and measuring performance, businesses can achieve significant results. Content marketing builds trust, drives organic traffic, generates leads, and supports other marketing efforts. Regularly review and refine your content strategy to stay ahead of trends, adapt to changes, and continuously improve your marketing efforts.

Chapter 5: Social Media Marketing

Introduction to Social Media Marketing

Social media marketing involves leveraging social media platforms to connect with your audience, build brand awareness, drive engagement, and achieve your marketing goals. With billions of active users on platforms like Facebook, Instagram, Twitter, LinkedIn, and Pinterest, social media marketing offers businesses a powerful way to reach a wide and diverse audience.

Social media marketing encompasses various activities, including content creation, community management, paid advertising, influencer partnerships, and social listening. In this chapter, we will explore the key components of social media marketing, including strategy development, platform selection, content creation, community management, advertising, and performance measurement.

The Importance of Social Media Marketing

Social media marketing is crucial for several reasons:

1. Widespread Reach: Social media platforms have billions of active users, providing businesses with the opportunity to reach a vast and diverse audience. By establishing a presence on social media, you can connect with potential customers, build brand awareness, and expand your reach.
2. Engagement and Interaction: Social media allows for direct interaction and engagement with your audience. You can respond to comments, answer questions, and participate in conversations, building stronger relationships with your customers.
3. Brand Loyalty: Consistent and meaningful engagement on social media can foster brand loyalty. By providing valuable content, addressing customer concerns, and showcasing your brand's personality, you can create a loyal community of followers.
4. Targeted Advertising: Social media advertising offers advanced targeting options, allowing you to reach specific demographics, interests, behaviors, and locations. This precision targeting ensures that your ads are seen by the most relevant audience, maximizing your advertising ROI.

5. Data and Insights: Social media platforms provide valuable data and insights into your audience's behavior, preferences, and interactions with your content. These insights can inform your marketing strategy, helping you create more effective campaigns.
6. Content Amplification: Social media is an excellent channel for amplifying your content and driving traffic to your website. By sharing your blog posts, videos, infographics, and other content on social media, you can increase its visibility and reach a broader audience.

Developing a Social Media Strategy

A social media strategy is a comprehensive plan that outlines how you will use social media platforms to achieve your marketing goals. Developing a social media strategy involves several key steps:

1. Define Your Goals: Clearly define the goals of your social media marketing strategy. Are you looking to increase brand awareness, drive traffic, generate leads, boost sales, or improve customer engagement? Your goals will guide your content planning, platform selection, and overall strategy. For example, if your goal is to generate leads, you might focus on creating lead magnets, such as ebooks and webinars, and promoting them through social media ads.
2. Understand Your Audience: Conduct audience research to understand your target audience's demographics, interests, behaviors, and pain points. Create buyer personas to represent different segments of your audience and tailor your social media content to their interests. For example, if your audience consists of young professionals, you might focus on LinkedIn and Instagram to reach them.
3. Choose the Right Platforms: Select the social media platforms that align with your goals and audience preferences. Each platform has its own unique features, user base, and content formats. For example, if your audience is primarily visual, you might prioritize Instagram and Pinterest. If you are targeting professionals, LinkedIn would be a suitable platform.
4. Create a Content Plan: Develop a content plan that outlines the types of content you will produce, the topics you will cover, and the publishing schedule. Your content plan should

align with your goals and audience preferences. For example, if your goal is to increase engagement, you might create interactive content such as polls, quizzes, and live videos.

5. Content Creation and Curation: Focus on creating high-quality, valuable, and engaging content that resonates with your audience. Mix original content with curated content from other sources to provide a diverse and valuable feed. Use a mix of content formats, such as images, videos, infographics, and articles, to keep your audience engaged.
6. Community Management: Actively manage your social media community by responding to comments, messages, and mentions. Engage with your audience by participating in conversations, asking questions, and encouraging user-generated content. Community management helps build stronger relationships with your audience and fosters brand loyalty.
7. Paid Advertising: Leverage social media advertising to amplify your content, reach a wider audience, and achieve specific marketing goals. Experiment with different ad formats, targeting options, and budgets to optimize your campaigns. Monitor and analyze ad performance to make data-driven decisions and improve your ROI.
8. Measure and Analyze Performance: Continuously measure and analyze the performance of your social media efforts to understand what's working, what's not, and how you can improve. Use analytics tools to track key metrics, such as reach, engagement, clicks, and conversions. Use these insights to refine your strategy and optimize your efforts for better results.

Tools for Developing a Social Media Strategy:

- Hootsuite (https://hootsuite.com/): A social media management tool that helps you plan, schedule, and analyze your social media content.
- Buffer (https://buffer.com/): A social media scheduling tool that helps you plan and promote your content across multiple platforms.
- Sprout Social (https://sproutsocial.com/): A social media management platform that provides tools for content planning, scheduling, and performance analysis.

- Google Analytics (https://analytics.google.com/): Provides insights into your social media traffic, user behavior, and conversion metrics.

Content Creation for Social Media

Creating engaging and valuable content is essential for social media marketing success. Your content should resonate with your audience, align with your goals, and leverage the unique features of each platform.

1. Understanding Platform-Specific Content: Each social media platform has its own unique features, content formats, and user preferences. Tailor your content to fit the platform you are using. For example, Instagram is a visual platform that prioritizes high-quality images and videos, while Twitter is suited for short, timely updates and conversations.
2. Visual Content: Visual content, such as images, videos, infographics, and GIFs, tends to perform well on social media. High-quality visuals capture attention, convey information effectively, and drive engagement. Use tools like Canva (https://www.canva.com/) and Adobe Creative Cloud (https://www.adobe.com/creativecloud.html) to create visually appealing content.
3. User-Generated Content (GPT-4o + You.com AI):User-Generated Content (UGC): UGC is content created by your audience, such as reviews, testimonials, photos, and videos. Encouraging your audience to share their experiences with your brand can build trust and authenticity. Feature UGC on your social media profiles and website to showcase real-life customer experiences. For example, GoPro frequently shares user-generated videos captured with their cameras, highlighting the product's capabilities and fostering a community of engaged users.
4. Interactive Content: Interactive content, such as polls, quizzes, live videos, and Q&A sessions, encourages audience participation and engagement. Interactive content can help you gather insights, foster community interaction, and keep your audience engaged. Instagram Stories and Facebook Live are excellent platforms for creating interactive content.
5. Stories and Short-Form Content: Stories and short-form content are ephemeral content formats that disappear after a set period (e.g., 24 hours). Platforms like Instagram, Facebook, and Snapchat offer Stories features that allow you to share behind-the-scenes

glimpses, time-sensitive updates, and interactive content. Stories can create a sense of urgency and encourage immediate engagement.

6. Educational and Informative Content: Provide valuable information and insights that educate your audience. This can include how-to guides, tutorials, industry news, and thought leadership content. Educational content positions your brand as an authority and helps build trust with your audience.

7. Consistent Branding: Maintain consistent branding across all your social media platforms. Use the same logo, color scheme, and tone of voice to create a cohesive brand identity. Consistent branding helps reinforce your brand message and makes your content easily recognizable.

Tools for Content Creation:

- Canva (https://www.canva.com/): A design tool for creating visually appealing graphics, infographics, and social media posts.
- Adobe Creative Cloud (https://www.adobe.com/creativecloud.html): A suite of professional design tools, including Photoshop, Illustrator, and Premiere Pro, for creating high-quality visual and video content.
- Animoto (https://animoto.com/): A video creation tool that helps you create engaging videos for social media.
- Buffer (https://buffer.com/): A social media scheduling tool that helps you plan and promote your content across multiple platforms.

Community Management

Community management involves actively engaging with your audience, responding to comments and messages, and fostering a positive and supportive community around your brand. Effective community management helps build stronger relationships with your audience and fosters brand loyalty.

1. Responding to Comments and Messages: Regularly monitor your social media profiles for comments, messages, and mentions. Respond promptly and thoughtfully to questions, feedback, and inquiries. Acknowledge positive comments and address negative feedback professionally and constructively.

2. Encouraging User Interaction: Encourage your audience to interact with your content by asking questions, running polls, and hosting Q&A sessions. Engaging with your audience in conversations helps build a sense of community and fosters deeper connections.
3. Handling Negative Feedback: Negative feedback is inevitable on social media. Handle it professionally and constructively by acknowledging the issue, apologizing if necessary, and offering a solution. Avoid deleting negative comments unless they violate community guidelines, as this can damage your brand's reputation.
4. Building Relationships with Influencers: Collaborate with influencers and industry experts to expand your reach and build credibility. Engage with influencers by commenting on their posts, sharing their content, and collaborating on projects. Influencers can help you reach new audiences and enhance your brand's reputation.
5. Creating a Community Space: Consider creating a dedicated community space, such as a Facebook Group or LinkedIn Group, where your audience can connect, share experiences, and engage with your brand. Actively participate in the community by sharing valuable content, answering questions, and facilitating discussions.

Tools for Community Management:

- Hootsuite (https://hootsuite.com/): A social media management tool that helps you monitor and respond to comments, messages, and mentions.
- Sprout Social (https://sproutsocial.com/): A social media management platform that provides tools for community management, engagement, and performance analysis.
- Buffer Reply (https://buffer.com/reply): A social media engagement tool that helps you manage and respond to comments and messages across multiple platforms.
- Facebook Groups (https://www.facebook.com/groups/): A platform for creating and managing community groups where your audience can connect and engage with your brand.

Social Media Advertising

Social media advertising involves promoting your content and products through paid ads on social media platforms. Social media ads offer advanced targeting options and can help you reach a wider audience, drive traffic, generate leads, and achieve specific marketing goals.

1. Choosing the Right Platforms: Select the social media platforms that align with your goals and audience preferences. Each platform offers unique ad formats and targeting options. For example, Facebook and Instagram are ideal for visual and video ads, while LinkedIn is suited for B2B advertising.
2. Creating Compelling Ad Content: Develop ad content that captures attention, conveys your message, and encourages action. Use high-quality visuals, compelling headlines, and clear calls-to-action (CTAs). Tailor your ad content to fit the unique features and audience preferences of each platform.
3. Targeting Your Audience: Leverage advanced targeting options to reach your ideal audience. Social media platforms offer various targeting options, including demographics, interests, behaviors, and custom audiences. Experiment with different targeting options to optimize your ad campaigns.
4. Setting Budgets and Bidding: Determine your ad budget and bidding strategy based on your goals and available resources. Social media platforms offer different bidding options, such as cost-per-click (CPC), cost-per-impression (CPM), and cost-per-action (CPA). Monitor your ad performance and adjust your budget and bidding strategy as needed.
5. A/B Testing: Conduct A/B testing to compare different ad variations and identify the most effective elements. Test different headlines, visuals, CTAs, and targeting options to optimize your ad campaigns. Use the insights from A/B testing to refine your ad content and improve performance.
6. Monitoring and Analyzing Performance: Continuously monitor and analyze the performance of your social media ads to understand what's working, what's not, and how you can improve. Use analytics tools to track key metrics, such as impressions, clicks, CTR, conversions, and ROI. Use these insights to make data-driven decisions and optimize your ad campaigns.

Tools for Social Media Advertising:

- Facebook Ads Manager (https://www.facebook.com/business/tools/ads-manager): A platform for creating, managing, and analyzing Facebook and Instagram ad campaigns.

- LinkedIn Campaign Manager (https://www.linkedin.com/campaignmanager): A platform for creating, managing, and analyzing LinkedIn ad campaigns.
- Twitter Ads (https://ads.twitter.com/): A platform for creating, managing, and analyzing Twitter ad campaigns.
- AdEspresso (https://adespresso.com/): A social media advertising tool that helps you create, manage, and optimize Facebook, Instagram, and Google Ads campaigns.

Measuring Social Media Performance

Measuring and analyzing the performance of your social media efforts is essential for understanding what's working, what's not, and how you can improve. By tracking key metrics and analyzing the data, you can make data-driven decisions and optimize your social media strategy for better results.

1. Reach and Impressions: Measure the number of unique users who see your content (reach) and the total number of times your content is displayed (impressions). High reach and impressions indicate that your content is visible to a large audience.
2. Engagement Metrics: Track how users interact with your content, including likes, shares, comments, and clicks. High engagement indicates that your content resonates with your audience and provides value.
3. Click-Through Rate (CTR): Measure the percentage of users who click on your content or ads. A high CTR indicates that your content is compelling and encourages action.
4. Conversion Metrics: Track the number of conversions generated through your social media efforts, such as sign-ups, purchases, or other desired actions. Use tools like Google Analytics (https://analytics.google.com/) to set up goals and track conversion rates.
5. ROI Metrics: Calculate the return on investment (ROI) of your social media efforts by comparing the revenue generated to the costs incurred. ROI helps you determine the financial effectiveness of your social media strategy and allocate resources accordingly.

Tools for Measuring Social Media Performance:

- Hootsuite Analytics (https://hootsuite.com/): Provides insights into your social media performance, including reach, engagement, and conversion metrics.

- Sprout Social (https://sproutsocial.com/): A social media management platform that offers comprehensive analytics and reporting features.
- Google Analytics (https://analytics.google.com/): Provides insights into your social media traffic, user behavior, and conversion metrics.
- Buffer Analyze (https://buffer.com/analyze): A social media analytics tool that helps you track and analyze your social media performance.

By regularly measuring and analyzing the performance of your social media efforts, you can gain valuable insights into what resonates with your audience and drives desired actions. Use these insights to refine your social media strategy, optimize your efforts, and achieve better results.

Real-World Examples of Successful Social Media Campaigns

Several companies have successfully leveraged social media marketing to achieve remarkable results. Here are a few notable examples:

1. Oreo's "Dunk in the Dark": During the 2013 Super Bowl, Oreo capitalized on a power outage by tweeting an image with the caption, "You can still dunk in the dark." The tweet quickly went viral, receiving thousands of retweets and likes. Oreo's timely and creative use of social media demonstrated the power of real-time marketing and the importance of agility in social media strategy. The campaign significantly boosted Oreo's brand visibility and engagement.
2. Airbnb's "#WeAccept": In response to global conversations around inclusivity and diversity, Airbnb launched the "#WeAccept" campaign. The campaign included a powerful Super Bowl ad and a commitment to provide short-term housing for 100,000 people in need. Airbnb used the hashtag #WeAccept across social media platforms to promote the message of acceptance and inclusivity. The campaign resonated with a wide audience, generating millions of impressions and fostering a sense of community and social responsibility.
3. Coca-Cola's "Share a Coke": Coca-Cola's "Share a Coke" campaign involved personalizing Coke bottles with popular names and encouraging consumers to share photos on social media using the hashtag #ShareaCoke. The campaign created a personal

connection with consumers and encouraged user-generated content. It was a massive success, leading to increased sales, widespread social media engagement, and a strengthened emotional connection between the brand and its consumers.

4. Old Spice's "The Man Your Man Could Smell Like": Old Spice revitalized its brand with the "The Man Your Man Could Smell Like" campaign, featuring humorous and memorable commercials starring Isaiah Mustafa. The campaign extended to social media, where Old Spice created personalized video responses to fans' comments and questions. The interactive and engaging approach resulted in viral success, significantly boosting brand awareness and sales.

5. GoPro's User-Generated Content Campaigns: GoPro has effectively utilized user-generated content (UGC) to promote its products. By encouraging users to share their GoPro-captured adventures and experiences on social media using the hashtag #GoPro, the company has built a strong community of engaged customers. GoPro frequently features the best UGC on its social media profiles and YouTube channel, showcasing the versatility and quality of its cameras. This strategy has helped GoPro generate authentic content, build trust, and foster brand loyalty.

Conclusion

Social media marketing is a powerful tool for connecting with your audience, building brand awareness, driving engagement, and achieving your marketing goals. By developing a comprehensive social media strategy, creating high-quality and engaging content, actively managing your community, leveraging paid advertising, and regularly measuring performance, businesses can achieve significant results. Social media marketing fosters direct interaction with your audience, builds brand loyalty, and provides valuable insights into audience behavior and preferences. Regularly review and refine your social media strategy to stay ahead of trends, adapt to changes, and continuously improve your marketing efforts.

Chapter 6: Email Marketing

Introduction to Email Marketing

Email marketing involves sending targeted and personalized emails to your audience to nurture relationships, promote products or services, and drive traffic to your website. Despite the rise of social media and other digital channels, email marketing remains one of the most effective and cost-efficient marketing strategies.

Email marketing allows businesses to communicate directly with their audience, deliver valuable content, and drive conversions. It provides a high return on investment (ROI) and offers advanced targeting and personalization options. In this chapter, we will explore the key components of email marketing, including building an email list, creating effective email campaigns, segmentation, automation, and performance measurement.

The Importance of Email Marketing

Email marketing is crucial for several reasons:

1. Direct Communication: Email allows for direct and personalized communication with your audience. Unlike social media, where algorithms control visibility, email ensures that your message reaches your subscribers' inboxes.
2. High ROI: Email marketing offers one of the highest returns on investment (ROI) among digital marketing channels. According to a study by the Data & Marketing Association (DMA), email marketing can yield an average ROI of $42 for every $1 spent.
3. Targeted and Personalized: Email marketing enables advanced targeting and personalization based on subscriber data, such as demographics, behavior, and preferences. Personalized emails are more relevant and engaging, leading to higher open rates, click-through rates, and conversions.
4. Nurtures Relationships: Email marketing helps nurture relationships with your audience by providing valuable content, addressing their needs, and maintaining consistent communication. Building strong relationships with your subscribers fosters brand loyalty and trust.

5. Measurable and Scalable: Email marketing provides detailed analytics and reporting features, allowing you to track key metrics, such as open rates, click-through rates, and conversions. These insights help you optimize your campaigns and achieve better results. Email marketing is also scalable, allowing you to reach a large audience without incurring significant additional costs.

Building an Email List

Building a high-quality email list is the foundation of successful email marketing. A high-quality list consists of engaged and interested subscribers who have opted in to receive your emails. There are several strategies for building an email list:

1. Opt-In Forms: Place opt-in forms on your website, blog, and landing pages to capture email addresses. Ensure that your forms are easy to find, visually appealing, and provide a clear value proposition. For example, you can offer a discount, free resource, or exclusive content in exchange for subscribing.
2. Lead Magnets: Offer valuable lead magnets, such as ebooks, whitepapers, checklists, webinars, and free trials, to incentivize subscriptions. Lead magnets should address your audience's needs and provide immediate value. Promote your lead magnets through your website, social media, and paid advertising.
3. Content Upgrades: Provide content upgrades on your blog posts and articles. A content upgrade is a piece of additional, valuable content related to the blog post that readers can access in exchange for their email address. For example, you can offer a downloadable checklist, template, or guide that complements the blog post.
4. Social Media: Promote your email list on your social media profiles and encourage your followers to subscribe. Use social media ads to drive traffic to your landing pages and opt-in forms. For example, you can run a Facebook ad campaign promoting a free ebook or webinar and capture email addresses through a dedicated landing page.
5. Webinars and Events: Host webinars, virtual events, and in-person events to capture email addresses. Require attendees to register with their email addresses to access the

event. Provide valuable content and insights during the event to build trust and encourage attendees to stay subscribed.
6. Exit-Intent Popups: Use exit-intent popups to capture email addresses when visitors are about to leave your website. Exit-intent popups can offer a discount, lead magnet, or exclusive content to incentivize subscriptions. Tools like OptinMonster (https://optinmonster.com/) and Sumo (https://sumo.com/) provide exit-intent popup features.
7. Referral Programs: Implement referral programs that encourage your existing subscribers to refer friends and family to join your email list. Offer incentives, such as discounts, freebies, or exclusive content, to both the referrer and the referred subscriber.

Tools for Building an Email List:

- Mailchimp (https://mailchimp.com/): An email marketing platform that provides tools for creating opt-in forms, landing pages, and lead magnets.
- ConvertKit (https://convertkit.com/): An email marketing tool designed for creators and bloggers, offering features for building and managing email lists.
- OptinMonster (https://optinmonster.com/): A lead generation tool that provides opt-in forms, popups, and exit-intent technology to capture email addresses.
- Sumo (https://sumo.com/): A suite of tools for website growth, including opt-in forms, popups, and social sharing features.

Creating Effective Email Campaigns

Creating effective email campaigns involves developing compelling content, designing visually appealing emails, and optimizing for deliverability and engagement.

1. Compelling Subject Lines: The subject line is the first thing subscribers see, and it significantly impacts open rates. Craft compelling and relevant subject lines that grab

attention and entice subscribers to open the email. Use personalization, urgency, and curiosity to make your subject lines stand out.

2. Engaging Email Content: Create engaging and valuable email content that addresses your subscribers' needs and interests. Use a conversational tone, personalize the content, and provide clear and actionable information. Include a mix of content types, such as articles, videos, infographics, and promotions, to keep your emails interesting.

3. Visually Appealing Design: Design visually appealing and mobile-responsive emails that enhance the user experience. Use a clean and organized layout, high-quality images, and consistent branding. Ensure that your emails are easy to read and navigate on both desktop and mobile devices.

4. Clear Call-to-Action (CTA): Include a clear and compelling call-to-action (CTA) in your emails that encourages subscribers to take the desired action. Use actionable language, such as "Download Now," "Shop Now," or "Learn More," and make the CTA button stand out with contrasting colors.

5. Personalization and Segmentation: Personalize your emails by addressing subscribers by name and tailoring the content to their preferences and behaviors. Use segmentation to divide your email list into smaller groups based on demographics, interests, and past interactions. Personalized and segmented emails are more relevant and engaging, leading to higher open rates and click-through rates.

6. A/B Testing: Conduct A/B testing to compare different email variations and identify the most effective elements. Test different subject lines, email content, CTAs, and design elements to optimize your campaigns. Use the insights from A/B testing to refine your email strategy and improve performance.

7. Optimizing for Deliverability: Ensure that your emails reach your subscribers' inboxes by optimizing for deliverability. Use a reputable email service provider (ESP), maintain a clean email list, and follow best practices for email authentication (e.g., SPF, DKIM, DMARC). Avoid spammy language and excessive use of images and links to reduce the risk of your emails being marked as spam. Monitor your sender's reputation and address any deliverability issues promptly.

Tools for Creating Effective Email Campaigns:

- Mailchimp (https://mailchimp.com/): An email marketing platform that offers tools for creating, sending, and analyzing email campaigns.
- ConvertKit (https://convertkit.com/): An email marketing tool designed for creators and bloggers, providing features for email design, automation, and personalization.
- ActiveCampaign (https://www.activecampaign.com/): An email marketing and automation platform that helps you create personalized email campaigns and workflows.
- Litmus (https://www.litmus.com/): An email testing and analytics tool that helps you optimize your emails for deliverability, design, and engagement.

Segmentation and Personalization

Segmentation and personalization are key to delivering relevant and engaging email content to your subscribers. By dividing your email list into smaller segments and tailoring your messages to each group, you can improve open rates, click-through rates, and conversions.

1. Segmentation: Segmentation involves dividing your email list into smaller groups based on specific criteria, such as demographics, interests, behavior, and past interactions. Common segmentation criteria include:
    - Demographics: Age, gender, location, income, etc.
    - Behavior: Purchase history, website activity, email engagement, etc.
    - Interests: Preferences, hobbies, topics of interest, etc.
    - Lifecycle Stage: New subscribers, loyal customers, inactive subscribers, etc.
2. For example, you might create separate segments for new subscribers and long-term customers, tailoring your messages to meet the unique needs and interests of each group.
3. Personalization: Personalization involves tailoring your email content to individual subscribers based on their preferences, behaviors, and interactions with your brand. Personalization techniques include:
    - Using the recipient's name: Address subscribers by their first name in the subject line and email content.

- Behavioral triggers: Send personalized emails based on specific actions, such as cart abandonment, product views, or downloads.
- Dynamic content: Use dynamic content blocks to display different content to different segments within the same email.
- Recommendations: Offer personalized product or content recommendations based on past behavior and preferences.

4. Personalization makes your emails more relevant and engaging, leading to higher open rates, click-through rates, and conversions.

Tools for Segmentation and Personalization:

- Mailchimp (https://mailchimp.com/): Offers advanced segmentation and personalization features to target specific subscriber groups and tailor your messages.
- ConvertKit (https://convertkit.com/): Provides tools for segmenting your email list and delivering personalized content to your subscribers.
- ActiveCampaign (https://www.activecampaign.com/): Offers robust segmentation and personalization features, including dynamic content and behavioral triggers.
- Klaviyo (https://www.klaviyo.com/): An email marketing platform that specializes in segmentation and personalization for e-commerce businesses.

Email Automation

Email automation involves setting up automated email workflows that are triggered by specific actions or events. Automation helps you deliver timely and relevant messages to your subscribers, nurture leads, and improve efficiency.

1. Welcome Series: Create a welcome series to introduce new subscribers to your brand, set expectations, and provide valuable information. A welcome series can include a thank-you email, a brand story, product highlights, and special offers.
2. Abandoned Cart Emails: Send automated emails to remind customers who have added products to their cart but haven't completed the purchase. Include product images, a clear CTA, and an incentive, such as a discount, to encourage them to complete their purchase.

3. Post-Purchase Follow-Up: Send follow-up emails after a purchase to thank customers, provide order details, and offer product recommendations. Follow-up emails can also include requests for reviews, feedback, and social media shares.
4. Re-Engagement Campaigns: Set up re-engagement campaigns to win back inactive subscribers. Send a series of emails with special offers, valuable content, and personalized messages to re-engage and retain your audience.
5. Lead Nurturing: Create automated workflows to nurture leads through the sales funnel. Provide valuable content, such as educational articles, case studies, and webinars, to guide leads toward making a purchase decision.
6. Birthday and Anniversary Emails: Send personalized emails to celebrate subscribers' birthdays and anniversaries. Include special offers, discounts, and personalized messages to make them feel valued and appreciated.

Tools for Email Automation:

- Mailchimp (https://mailchimp.com/): Offers automation features for creating welcome series, abandoned cart emails, and other automated workflows.
- ActiveCampaign (https://www.activecampaign.com/): Provides advanced automation tools for creating personalized email workflows and lead nurturing campaigns.
- Drip (https://www.drip.com/): An email marketing automation platform designed for e-commerce businesses, offering features for abandoned cart emails, post-purchase follow-ups, and more.
- HubSpot (https://www.hubspot.com/): An all-in-one marketing platform that includes email automation features for lead nurturing, segmentation, and personalization.

Measuring Email Marketing Performance

Measuring and analyzing the performance of your email marketing efforts is essential for understanding what's working, what's not, and how you can improve. By tracking key metrics and analyzing data, you can make data-driven decisions and optimize your email campaigns for better results.

1. Open Rate: The percentage of recipients who open your email. A high open rate indicates that your subject lines are compelling and relevant to your audience. Monitor your open rates and test different subject lines to improve performance.
2. Click-Through Rate (CTR): The percentage of recipients who click on a link within your email. A high CTR indicates that your email content and CTAs are engaging and encourage action. Monitor your CTR and test different content, CTAs, and design elements to optimize performance.
3. Conversion Rate: The percentage of recipients who complete a desired action, such as making a purchase, filling out a form, or downloading a resource. Conversion rate is a key indicator of the effectiveness of your email campaigns in driving valuable actions. Monitor your conversion rates and optimize your email content and CTAs to improve performance.
4. Bounce Rate: The percentage of emails that are not delivered successfully to recipients' inboxes. A high bounce rate can indicate issues with your email list quality or deliverability. Monitor your bounce rates and clean your email list regularly to maintain a healthy sender reputation.
5. Unsubscribe Rate: The percentage of recipients who unsubscribe from your email list. A high unsubscribe rate may indicate that your emails are not relevant or valuable to your audience. Monitor your unsubscribe rates and ensure that you are delivering relevant and engaging content to your subscribers.
6. ROI: Calculate the return on investment (ROI) of your email marketing efforts by comparing the revenue generated to the costs incurred. ROI helps you determine the financial effectiveness of your email campaigns and allocate resources accordingly.

Tools for Measuring Email Marketing Performance:

- Mailchimp (https://mailchimp.com/): Provides detailed analytics and reporting features to track key email marketing metrics.
- ConvertKit (https://convertkit.com/): Offers performance tracking tools to measure open rates, click-through rates, and conversions.
- ActiveCampaign (https://www.activecampaign.com/): Provides comprehensive analytics and reporting features to monitor email performance and optimize campaigns.
- Litmus (https://www.litmus.com/): An email testing and analytics tool that helps you optimize your emails for deliverability, design, and engagement.

Real-World Examples of Successful Email Marketing Campaigns

Several companies have successfully leveraged email marketing to achieve remarkable results. Here are a few notable examples:

1. BuzzFeed: BuzzFeed's email newsletters are known for their engaging and personalized content. The company segments its email list based on subscribers' interests and behaviors, delivering relevant articles, quizzes, and videos. BuzzFeed's entertaining and valuable content has helped the company build a loyal audience and drive significant traffic to its website.
2. Charity: Water: Charity: Water, a nonprofit organization, uses email marketing to keep donors informed and engaged. The organization sends personalized updates on the impact of donations, including stories, photos, and videos of completed water projects. By showing the tangible results of donations, Charity: Water fosters donor loyalty and encourages continued support.
3. Sephora: Sephora, a beauty retailer, uses email marketing to deliver personalized product recommendations, promotions, and beauty tips. The company segments its email list based on customers' purchase history, preferences, and behavior. Sephora's targeted and personalized emails drive engagement and encourage repeat purchases.
4. Grammarly: Grammarly, a writing assistant tool, uses email marketing to onboard new users, provide usage tips, and promote premium features. The company sends a series of

onboarding emails to help new users get started and maximize the tool's benefits. Grammarly's informative and helpful emails improve user retention and drive conversions to premium plans.

5. Spotify: Spotify, a music streaming service, uses personalized email campaigns to engage users and promote new music. The company sends personalized playlists, concert recommendations, and updates based on users' listening habits. Spotify's personalized and relevant emails enhance the user experience and drive engagement.

Conclusion

Email marketing is a powerful and cost-effective strategy for nurturing relationships, promoting products or services, and driving conversions. By building a high-quality email list, creating compelling email campaigns, leveraging segmentation and personalization, implementing automation, and regularly measuring performance, businesses can achieve significant results. Email marketing offers direct communication with your audience, a high ROI, and advanced targeting options. Regularly review and refine your email strategy to stay ahead of trends, adapt to changes, and continuously improve your marketing efforts. The following sections will delve deeper into specific aspects of email marketing and provide actionable insights to help you maximize your results.

Chapter 7: Pay-Per-Click (PPC) Advertising

Introduction to PPC Advertising

Pay-Per-Click (PPC) advertising is a model of digital marketing where advertisers pay a fee each time one of their ads is clicked. Essentially, it's a way of buying visits to your site rather than attempting to earn those visits organically. PPC advertising is commonly used on platforms like Google Ads, Bing Ads, Facebook Ads, and LinkedIn Ads.

PPC can drive immediate traffic to your website and is especially useful for promoting time-sensitive offers, targeting specific audience segments, and testing marketing strategies. In this chapter, we will explore the key components of PPC advertising, including campaign setup, keyword research, ad creation, bidding strategies, and performance measurement.

The Importance of PPC Advertising

PPC advertising is crucial for several reasons:

1. Immediate Results: PPC campaigns can generate traffic and leads almost immediately after launch. This is particularly beneficial for new websites, product launches, and time-sensitive promotions.
2. Targeted Advertising: PPC platforms offer advanced targeting options, allowing you to reach specific demographics, interests, and behaviors. You can also target users based on their search queries, location, device, and time of day.
3. Budget Control: PPC advertising provides flexibility in budgeting. You can set daily or monthly budgets, control your bids, and adjust spending based on performance. This allows for cost-effective marketing that can be scaled according to your resources.
4. Measurable Results: PPC platforms offer detailed analytics and reporting features, enabling you to track key metrics such as impressions, clicks, CTR, conversions, and ROI. This data helps you make informed decisions and optimize your campaigns for better performance.

5. Complementary to SEO: PPC can complement your SEO efforts by providing immediate visibility while your organic rankings improve. It can also help you identify high-performing keywords that you can target in your SEO strategy.

Setting Up a PPC Campaign

Setting up a successful PPC campaign involves several key steps:

1. Defining Goals: Clearly define the goals of your PPC campaign. Are you looking to drive traffic, generate leads, increase sales, or promote brand awareness? Your goals will guide your campaign setup, targeting, and optimization strategies.
2. Choosing the Right Platform: Select the PPC platform that aligns with your goals and audience preferences. Popular PPC platforms include Google Ads, Bing Ads, Facebook Ads, LinkedIn Ads, and Twitter Ads. Each platform offers unique features and targeting options.
3. Keyword Research: Conduct keyword research to identify the search terms and phrases that your target audience is using. Use tools like Google Keyword Planner (https://ads.google.com/home/tools/keyword-planner/), Ahrefs (https://ahrefs.com/), and SEMrush (https://www.semrush.com/) to generate keyword ideas, analyze search volume, competition, and cost-per-click (CPC).
4. Creating Ad Groups: Organize your keywords into ad groups based on common themes or topics. Each ad group should contain a set of related keywords and corresponding ads. This structure helps ensure that your ads are relevant to the search queries and improves your Quality Score.
5. Writing Ad Copy: Craft compelling ad copy that includes your target keywords, highlights your unique value proposition, and includes a clear call-to-action (CTA). Use ad extensions to provide additional information and enhance your ad's visibility.
6. Setting Bids and Budgets: Determine your bidding strategy and set your maximum bids for each keyword. Choose between manual bidding, where you set bids for individual keywords, or automated bidding, where the platform adjusts bids based on your goals. Set daily or monthly budgets to control your ad spend.

7. Creating Landing Pages: Design landing pages that are relevant to your ads and optimized for conversions. Ensure that your landing pages provide a clear and compelling message, match the ad copy, and include a strong CTA. Optimize for mobile devices and ensure fast loading times.

Tools for PPC Campaign Setup:

- Google Ads (https://ads.google.com/): A PPC platform that allows you to create search, display, video, and shopping ads.
- Bing Ads (https://ads.microsoft.com/): A PPC platform for creating search and shopping ads on the Bing search engine.
- Facebook Ads Manager (https://www.facebook.com/business/tools/ads-manager): A platform for creating and managing Facebook and Instagram ad campaigns.
- LinkedIn Campaign Manager (https://www.linkedin.com/campaignmanager): A platform for creating and managing LinkedIn ad campaigns.

Bidding Strategies

Bidding strategies play a crucial role in the success of your PPC campaigns. The right strategy can help you achieve your goals while staying within your budget. Common bidding strategies include:

1. Manual CPC Bidding: You set the maximum cost-per-click (CPC) for your ads. This gives you full control over your bids but requires ongoing management to optimize performance.
2. Enhanced CPC (ECPC): A semi-automated bidding strategy where you set the base bid, and the platform adjusts it to maximize conversions. ECPC uses historical data to make bid adjustments.
3. Maximize Clicks: An automated bidding strategy that aims to get the maximum number of clicks within your budget. This strategy is useful for driving traffic to your website.
4. Target CPA (Cost Per Acquisition): An automated bidding strategy that aims to achieve a target cost per acquisition. The platform adjusts bids to generate conversions at or below your target CPA.

5. Target ROAS (Return on Ad Spend): An automated bidding strategy that aims to achieve a target return on ad spend. The platform adjusts bids to maximize revenue while maintaining your target ROAS.
6. Maximize Conversions: An automated bidding strategy that aims to get the maximum number of conversions within your budget. This strategy uses historical data to optimize bids for conversions.
7. Target Impression Share: An automated bidding strategy that aims to achieve a certain percentage of ad impressions. This strategy is useful for brand awareness campaigns.

Tools for Bidding Strategies:

- Google Ads (https://ads.google.com/): Offers various bidding strategies, including manual CPC, ECPC, maximize clicks, target CPA, target ROAS, and maximize conversions.
- Bing Ads (https://ads.microsoft.com/): Provides bidding options similar to Google Ads, including manual CPC, enhanced CPC, and automated bidding strategies.
- Facebook Ads Manager (https://www.facebook.com/business/tools/ads-manager): Offers bidding options such as manual bidding, automatic bidding, and target cost bidding.

Measuring PPC Performance

Measuring and analyzing the performance of your PPC campaigns is essential for understanding what's working, what's not, and how you can improve. By tracking key metrics and analyzing data, you can make data-driven decisions and optimize your PPC campaigns for better results.

1. Impressions: The number of times your ad is displayed. High impressions indicate that your ads are being seen by a large audience.
2. Clicks: The number of times users click on your ad. Clicks indicate that your ad is relevant and engaging to users.

3. Click-Through Rate (CTR): The percentage of clicks your ad receives relative to the number of impressions. A high CTR indicates that your ad copy and targeting are effective.
4. Cost Per Click (CPC): The average amount you pay for each click on your ad. CPC helps you understand the cost-efficiency of your campaigns.
5. Conversions: The number of desired actions completed by users, such as purchases, sign-ups, or downloads. Conversions are a key indicator of the effectiveness of your PPC campaigns.
6. Cost Per Acquisition (CPA): The average cost of acquiring a new customer or lead. CPA helps you understand the cost-efficiency of your campaigns in generating conversions.
7. Return on Ad Spend (ROAS): The revenue generated for every dollar spent on advertising. ROAS helps you evaluate the overall effectiveness and profitability of your PPC campaigns.
8. Quality Score: A metric used by Google Ads to measure the relevance and quality of your keywords, ads, and landing pages. A high Quality Score can lead to lower CPCs and better ad positions.

Tools for Measuring PPC Performance:

- Google Ads (https://ads.google.com/): Provides detailed analytics and reporting features to track key PPC metrics.
- Bing Ads (https://ads.microsoft.com/): Offers performance tracking tools similar to Google Ads, including impressions, clicks, CTR, conversions, and more.
- Facebook Ads Manager (https://www.facebook.com/business/tools/ads-manager): Provides insights into ad performance, including reach, engagement, clicks, and conversions.
- SEMrush (https://www.semrush.com/): An all-in-one marketing tool that offers PPC performance tracking, keyword research, and competitor analysis.

Real-World Examples of Successful PPC Campaigns

Several companies have successfully leveraged PPC advertising to achieve remarkable results. Here are a few notable examples:

1. Amazon: Amazon uses PPC advertising on both Google Ads and its own platform, Amazon Advertising, to promote products and drive sales. By targeting relevant keywords and using a combination of manual and automated bidding strategies, Amazon effectively reaches potential customers and drives conversions. Amazon's PPC campaigns are known for their high ROI and significant contribution to overall sales.
2. REI: REI, an outdoor retail company, uses PPC advertising to promote its products and seasonal sales. By targeting relevant keywords and using compelling ad copy, REI drives traffic to its website and increases online sales. The company also uses retargeting ads to reach userswho have previously visited their website, reminding them of the products they viewed and encouraging them to complete their purchase. REI's PPC campaigns effectively boost brand visibility, drive traffic, and increase conversions.
3. Slack: Slack, a collaboration and communication platform, leverages PPC advertising to generate leads and drive sign-ups for its service. Slack uses a combination of search, display, and video ads to target businesses and professionals. By using compelling ad copy, clear CTAs, and targeted landing pages, Slack successfully captures leads and drives conversions. The company's data-driven approach to PPC advertising helps optimize campaigns for maximum ROI.
4. Grammarly: Grammarly, a writing assistant tool, uses PPC advertising to attract new users and promote its premium plans. Grammarly runs search and display ads on platforms like Google Ads and Bing Ads, targeting relevant keywords and audiences. The company uses a combination of manual and automated bidding strategies to maximize click-through rates and conversions. Grammarly's PPC campaigns are known for their precision targeting and high ROI.
5. HubSpot: HubSpot, a provider of inbound marketing and sales software, uses PPC advertising to generate leads and drive traffic to its content and resources. HubSpot runs search and display ads, targeting keywords related to marketing, sales, and customer service. The company uses lead magnets, such as ebooks, webinars, and free tools, to capture email addresses and nurture leads. HubSpot's data-driven PPC strategy helps achieve high conversion rates and significant ROI.

Conclusion

PPC advertising is a powerful and versatile digital marketing strategy that can drive immediate traffic, generate leads, and increase sales. By setting up well-structured campaigns, conducting thorough keyword research, creating compelling ads, optimizing bids, and regularly measuring performance, businesses can achieve significant results. PPC offers advanced targeting options, budget control, and measurable results, making it an essential component of a comprehensive digital marketing strategy. Regularly review and refine your PPC strategy to stay ahead of trends, adapt to changes, and continuously improve your marketing efforts.

Chapter 8: Influencer Marketing

Introduction to Influencer Marketing

Influencer marketing involves partnering with individuals who have a large and engaged following on social media or other online platforms to promote your brand, products, or services. Influencers can help you reach a wider audience, build credibility, and drive engagement. Influencer marketing leverages the trust and influence that these individuals have with their followers to achieve marketing goals.

In this chapter, we will explore the key components of influencer marketing, including identifying the right influencers, building relationships, creating effective campaigns, and measuring performance.

The Importance of Influencer Marketing

Influencer marketing is crucial for several reasons:

1. **Reach and Exposure:** Influencers have dedicated and engaged followers who trust their recommendations. Partnering with influencers can help you reach a larger audience and increase brand exposure.
2. **Credibility and Trust:** Influencers have built credibility and trust with their followers. When they endorse your brand or products, it carries more weight and can influence purchasing decisions.
3. **Engagement:** Influencers create content that resonates with their audience, leading to higher engagement rates. Collaborating with influencers can drive more likes, comments, shares, and overall interaction with your brand.
4. **Targeted Marketing:** Influencers often have niche audiences with specific interests. Partnering with influencers who align with your brand allows you to target a highly relevant audience.
5. **Content Creation:** Influencers are skilled content creators who can produce high-quality and authentic content for your brand. This content can be repurposed across your marketing channels.

Identifying the Right Influencers

Identifying the right influencers involves finding individuals who align with your brand values, target audience, and marketing goals. Consider the following factors when selecting influencers:

1. Relevance: Ensure that the influencer's content and audience align with your brand and industry. The influencer should share similar values and interests with your target audience.
2. Reach: Evaluate the size of the influencer's following. While larger followings can provide more exposure, micro-influencers (with smaller but highly engaged audiences) can also be effective.
3. Engagement: Analyze the influencer's engagement rates, including likes, comments, shares, and overall interaction with their content. High engagement indicates a strong connection with their audience.
4. Authenticity: Look for influencers who create authentic and genuine content. Authentic influencers are more likely to build trust with their audience and provide credible endorsements.
5. Content Quality: Assess the quality of the influencer's content, including visuals, writing, and overall presentation. High-quality content reflects positively on your brand.
6. Past Collaborations: Review the influencer's past collaborations with other brands. Evaluate the success and impact of these partnerships to gauge the influencer's effectiveness.

Tools for Identifying Influencers:

- BuzzSumo (https://buzzsumo.com/): Helps you find influencers in your industry and analyze their engagement and reach.
- Upfluence (https://www.upfluence.com/): An influencer marketing platform that offers tools for influencer discovery, relationship management, and campaign tracking.
- NinjaOutreach (https://ninjaoutreach.com/): Provides influencer search and outreach tools to help you find and connect with influencers.
- Traackr (https://www.traackr.com/): An influencer marketing platform that helps you discover, manage, and measure influencer relationships.

Building Relationships with Influencers

Building strong and mutually beneficial relationships with influencers is key to successful influencer marketing. Follow these steps to establish and maintain positive relationships:

1. Research and Approach: Conduct thorough research to understand the influencer's content, values, and audience. Personalize your outreach by referencing specific content or posts that you admire. Clearly explain why you want to collaborate and how it can benefit both parties.
2. Offer Value: Provide value to the influencer by offering fair compensation, exclusive access to products, or opportunities for growth. Consider offering commission-based incentives or affiliate programs to encourage ongoing collaboration.
3. Set Clear Expectations: Communicate your campaign goals, deliverables, timelines, and any specific requirements. Ensure that both parties are aligned on expectations and agree on the terms of the collaboration.
4. Respect Creative Freedom: Allow influencers to create content in their unique style and voice. Trust their expertise and creativity to produce authentic and engaging content that resonates with their audience.
5. Maintain Communication: Keep the lines of communication open throughout the collaboration. Provide feedback, answer questions, and address any concerns promptly. Building a positive and respectful relationship can lead to long-term partnerships.
6. Show Appreciation: Acknowledge and appreciate the influencer's efforts and contributions. Share their content on your channels, give them shoutouts, and express gratitude for their collaboration.

Creating Effective Influencer Marketing Campaigns

Creating successful influencer marketing campaigns involves strategic planning, clear communication, and effective execution. Follow these steps to create impactful campaigns:

1. Define Campaign Goals: Clearly define the goals of your influencer marketing campaign. Are you looking to increase brand awareness, drive traffic, generate leads, or boost sales? Your goals will guide your campaign strategy and metrics for success.
2. Develop a Campaign Brief: Create a detailed campaign brief that outlines your goals, target audience, key messages, deliverables, timelines, and any specific requirements. Provide influencers with the necessary information and resources to create content aligned with your brand.
3. Collaborate on Content: Work closely with influencers to brainstorm and develop content ideas that resonate with their audience and align with your campaign goals. Encourage influencers to share their creative input and ensure that the content is authentic and engaging.
4. Leverage Multiple Platforms: Utilize various social media platforms to maximize the reach and impact of your campaign. Consider using a mix of Instagram, YouTube, TikTok, Twitter, and blogs to reach different audience segments.
5. Track and Measure Performance: Monitor the performance of your influencer marketing campaign by tracking key metrics such as reach, engagement, clicks, conversions, and ROI. Use tools like Google Analytics, social media analytics, and influencer marketing platforms to gather data and insights.
6. Analyze and Optimize: Analyze the results of your campaign to understand what worked and what didn't. Use these insights to optimize future campaigns and improve your influencer marketing strategy.

Tools for Influencer Marketing Campaigns:

- Upfluence (https://www.upfluence.com/): Offers tools for influencer discovery, relationship management, and campaign tracking.
- NinjaOutreach (https://ninjaoutreach.com/): Provides influencer search and outreach tools to help you find and connect with influencers.
- Traackr (https://www.traackr.com/): An influencer marketing platform that helps you discover, manage, and measure influencer relationships.
- Hootsuite (https://hootsuite.com/): A social media management tool that offers analytics and reporting features to track the performance of your influencer campaigns.

Measuring Influencer Marketing Performance

Measuring and analyzing the performance of your influencer marketing campaigns is essential for understanding their impact and ROI. By tracking key metrics and analyzing the data, you can make data-driven decisions and optimize your influencer marketing strategy.

1. Reach: Measure the total number of unique users who have seen the influencer's content. High reach indicates that your campaign has reached a large audience.
2. Engagement: Track the number of likes, comments, shares, and overall interaction with the influencer's content. High engagement indicates that the content resonates with the audience and drives interaction.
3. Click-Through Rate (CTR): Measure the percentage of users who click on links or CTAs within the influencer's content. A high CTR indicates that the content effectively drives traffic to your website or landing page.
4. Conversions: Track the number of desired actions completed by users, such as purchases, sign-ups, or downloads. Conversions are a key indicator of the effectiveness of your influencer marketing campaign in driving valuable actions.
5. Return on Investment (ROI): Calculate the ROI of your influencer marketing campaign by comparing the revenue generated to the costs incurred. ROI helps you determine the financial effectiveness and profitability of your influencer partnerships.

6. Brand Sentiment: Analyze the sentiment of the comments and feedback on the influencer's content. Positive brand sentiment indicates that the campaign has resonated well with the audience and has enhanced your brand's reputation.
7. Traffic: Use tools like Google Analytics to track the amount of traffic driven to your website or landing page from the influencer's content. Analyze the behavior of these visitors to understand their engagement and conversion patterns.

Tools for Measuring Influencer Marketing Performance:

- Google Analytics (https://analytics.google.com/): Provides insights into website traffic, user behavior, and conversion metrics.
- Hootsuite Analytics (https://hootsuite.com/): Offers analytics and reporting features to track social media performance, including influencer campaigns.
- Traackr (https://www.traackr.com/): An influencer marketing platform that provides tools for tracking and measuring influencer campaign performance.
- Upfluence (https://www.upfluence.com/): Offers performance tracking features to measure the impact and ROI of your influencer marketing campaigns.
- Sprout Social (https://sproutsocial.com/): A social media management platform that provides comprehensive analytics and reporting features.

Real-World Examples of Successful Influencer Marketing Campaigns

Several brands have successfully leveraged influencer marketing to achieve remarkable results. Here are a few notable examples:

1. Daniel Wellington: Daniel Wellington, a watch brand, built its entire business model around influencer marketing. The brand partnered with a wide range of influencers, from micro-influencers to celebrities, to promote its watches on social media. Influencers shared photos of themselves wearing Daniel Wellington watches and provided discount codes to their followers. This strategy helped Daniel Wellington rapidly grow its brand awareness, increase sales, and build a strong social media presence.
2. Glossier: Glossier, a beauty brand, uses influencer marketing to foster a sense of community and authenticity. The brand collaborates with beauty influencers, makeup

artists, and everyday users to share their experiences with Glossier products. By featuring real people and authentic reviews, Glossier builds trust and credibility with its audience. The brand also encourages user-generated content and regularly features customers on its social media channels.

3. Gymshark: Gymshark, a fitness apparel brand, leverages influencer marketing to connect with fitness enthusiasts and athletes. The brand partners with fitness influencers and athletes to promote its products through workout videos, tutorials, and motivational content. Gymshark's influencer partnerships help create a strong sense of community and brand loyalty among fitness enthusiasts.

4. Fiji Water: Fiji Water executed a successful influencer marketing campaign during the 2019 Golden Globe Awards. The brand hired a model, known as the "Fiji Water Girl," to photobomb celebrities on the red carpet while holding Fiji Water bottles. The photos went viral on social media, generating millions of impressions and significant media coverage. This creative and unexpected campaign boosted Fiji Water's brand visibility and engagement.

5. ASOS: ASOS, an online fashion retailer, uses influencer marketing to showcase its latest collections and trends. The brand collaborates with fashion influencers and bloggers to create stylish and aspirational content featuring ASOS products. Influencers share outfit photos, styling tips, and shopping hauls with their followers, driving traffic to the ASOS website and increasing sales.

Conclusion

Influencer marketing is a powerful strategy for reaching a wider audience, building credibility, and driving engagement. By identifying the right influencers, building strong relationships, creating effective campaigns, and measuring performance, businesses can achieve significant results. Influencer marketing leverages the trust and influence that individuals have with their followers to promote your brand and achieve marketing goals. Regularly review and refine your influencer marketing strategy to stay ahead of trends, adapt to changes, and continuously improve your marketing efforts.

Chapter 9: Content Optimization and SEO

Introduction to Content Optimization and SEO

Content optimization and Search Engine Optimization (SEO) involve improving the quality and relevance of your content to rank higher in search engine results pages (SERPs) and attract organic traffic. By optimizing your content for search engines and users, you can increase visibility, drive traffic, and improve engagement.

In this chapter, we will explore the key components of content optimization and SEO, including keyword research, on-page optimization, technical SEO, content creation, and performance measurement.

The Importance of Content Optimization and SEO

Content optimization and SEO are crucial for several reasons:

1. Increased Visibility: Higher rankings in search engine results pages lead to increased visibility and exposure to potential customers. Most users tend to click on the top results, so ranking higher can significantly boost your website traffic.
2. Organic Traffic: Organic traffic is the most valuable type of traffic because it is highly targeted and cost-effective. Unlike paid advertising, organic traffic doesn't require ongoing payments, making it a sustainable long-term strategy.
3. Credibility and Trust: Websites that rank higher in search results are often perceived as more credible and trustworthy by users. Achieving high rankings can enhance your brand's reputation and authority in your industry.
4. User Experience: SEO involves optimizing your website's structure, speed, and usability, which improves the overall user experience. A well-optimized website is easier to navigate, loads quickly, and provides valuable content, leading to higher user satisfaction.
5. Competitive Advantage: SEO provides a competitive advantage by helping you outrank competitors and capture a larger share of organic traffic. A strong SEO strategy can differentiate your brand and position you as a leader in your industry.

Keyword Research

Keyword research is the foundation of SEO. It involves identifying the search terms and phrases that users enter into search engines when looking for information, products, or services related to your business. By targeting the right keywords, you can attract relevant traffic to your website and improve your chances of ranking higher in search results.

1. Identifying Relevant Keywords: Start by brainstorming a list of topics and terms related to your business. Think about the words and phrases your target audience might use when searching for your products or services. Use tools like Google Keyword Planner (https://ads.google.com/home/tools/keyword-planner/), Ahrefs (https://ahrefs.com/), and SEMrush (https://www.semrush.com/) to generate keyword ideas and identify search volume, competition, and keyword difficulty.

2. Long-Tail Keywords: Long-tail keywords are longer, more specific phrases that typically have lower search volume but higher conversion potential. While short-tail keywords (e.g., "shoes") are highly competitive, long-tail keywords (e.g., "best running shoes for flat feet") are less competitive and more targeted. Incorporating long-tail keywords into your SEO strategy can help you attract highly relevant traffic and improve your chances of ranking.

3. Analyzing Competitor Keywords: Analyzing your competitors' keywords can provide valuable insights into their SEO strategies and help you identify opportunities. Use tools like Ahrefs (https://ahrefs.com/), SEMrush (https://www.semrush.com/), and SpyFu (https://www.spyfu.com/) to discover the keywords your competitors are ranking for, their search volumes, and their backlink profiles. This information can help you refine your keyword strategy and target keywords that your competitors may have overlooked.

4. Keyword Intent: Understanding the intent behind a keyword is crucial for creating content that meets user expectations. There are four main types of keyword intent: informational (e.g., "how to fix a leaky faucet"), navigational (e.g., "Facebook login"), transactional (e.g., "buy running shoes"), and commercial investigation (e.g., "best running shoes 2024"). By aligning your content with the user's intent, you can improve user engagement and increase the likelihood of ranking higher in search results.

Tools for Keyword Research:

- Google Keyword Planner (https://ads.google.com/home/tools/keyword-planner/): Provides keyword ideas, search volume, and competition data.
- Ahrefs (https://ahrefs.com/): An SEO tool for keyword research, competitor analysis, and performance tracking.
- SEMrush (https://www.semrush.com/): An all-in-one SEO tool for keyword research, competitor analysis, and performance tracking.
- SpyFu (https://www.spyfu.com/): Provides competitor keyword analysis and insights into their PPC and SEO strategies.

On-Page Optimization

On-page optimization involves optimizing individual pages on your website to rank higher in search results and attract relevant traffic. This includes optimizing content, HTML source code, and overall user experience. Key elements of on-page optimization include:

1. Title Tags: The title tag is an HTML element that specifies the title of a web page. It is displayed on search engine results pages (SERPs) as the clickable headline. Title tags should be unique, descriptive, and include the target keyword. Keep the title length between 50-60 characters to ensure it displays properly in search results.
2. Meta Descriptions: The meta description is an HTML element that provides a brief summary of a web page. It appears below the title tag in search results and can influence click-through rates. Meta descriptions should be compelling, informative, and include the target keyword. Keep the description length between 150-160 characters.
3. Header Tags (H1, H2, H3, etc.): Header tags help structure your content and make it easier for search engines and users to understand the hierarchy of information. The H1 tag should include the primary keyword and serve as the main heading of the page. Use H2, H3, and other header tags to break down content into logical sections and sub-

sections. This not only improves readability but also helps search engines understand the structure and relevance of your content.

4. URL Structure: URLs should be short, descriptive, and include the target keyword. Avoid using special characters, numbers, and unnecessary words. Clean and user-friendly URLs improve click-through rates and make it easier for search engines to crawl and index your pages.

5. Content Optimization: High-quality, relevant, and engaging content is crucial for SEO. Ensure that your content provides value to users, addresses their needs, and answers their questions. Use the target keyword naturally throughout the content, including in the introduction, body, and conclusion. Avoid keyword stuffing, as it can harm your rankings.

6. Internal Linking: Internal links connect different pages on your website and help search engines understand the structure and hierarchy of your content. They also improve user experience by guiding visitors to relevant pages. Use descriptive anchor text and link to relevant pages to enhance your internal linking strategy.

7. Image Optimization: Images enhance the visual appeal of your content and improve user engagement. Optimize images by using descriptive file names, adding alt text, and compressing file sizes to improve loading times. Alt text should describe the image and include the target keyword when relevant.

Tools for On-Page Optimization:

- Yoast SEO (https://yoast.com/): A WordPress plugin that helps optimize your content for search engines by providing real-time feedback and recommendations.
- Moz On-Page Grader (https://moz.com/products/pro/on-page-grader): Analyzes your web pages and provides actionable insights to improve on-page optimization.
- Screaming Frog (https://www.screamingfrog.co.uk/seo-spider/): A website crawler that helps identify on-page SEO issues, such as broken links, duplicate content, and missing meta tags.
- Google Search Console (https://search.google.com/search-console/): Provides insights into your website's performance, crawl errors, and indexing status.

Technical SEO

Technical SEO involves optimizing the technical aspects of your website to improve its crawlability, indexability, and overall performance. Key elements of technical SEO include:

1. Website Speed: Page load speed is a critical ranking factor and directly impacts user experience. Slow-loading pages can lead to higher bounce rates and lower rankings. Optimize your website's speed by compressing images, minifying CSS and JavaScript files, leveraging browser caching, and using a content delivery network (CDN).
2. Mobile-Friendliness: With the increasing use of mobile devices, having a mobile-friendly website is essential for SEO. Ensure that your website is responsive and provides a seamless experience across all devices. Use Google's Mobile-Friendly Test (https://search.google.com/test/mobile-friendly) to check your website's mobile compatibility.
3. XML Sitemap: An XML sitemap is a file that lists all the important pages on your website and helps search engines crawl and index your content. Submit your XML sitemap to Google Search Console (https://search.google.com/search-console/) and Bing Webmaster Tools (https://www.bing.com/toolbox/webmaster) to ensure that search engines can discover and index your pages.
4. Robots.txt: The robots.txt file is used to control which pages search engines can and cannot crawl. Ensure that your robots.txt file is correctly configured and does not block important pages from being indexed.
5. Secure Website (HTTPS): Secure websites (HTTPS) are preferred by search engines and users. Install an SSL certificate to encrypt data and ensure that your website is secure. Google considers HTTPS as a ranking signal, so having a secure website can positively impact your rankings.
6. Structured Data and Schema Markup: Structured data and schema markup help search engines understand the content and context of your web pages. Implementing schema markup can enhance your search results with rich snippets, such as star ratings, reviews, and event details. Use Google's Structured Data Markup Helper (https://www.google.com/webmasters/markup-helper/) to generate and test schema markup for your website.

Tools for Technical SEO:

- Google PageSpeed Insights (https://developers.google.com/speed/pagespeed/insights/): Analyzes your website's speed and provides recommendations for improvement.
- GTmetrix (https://gtmetrix.com/): A website performance testing tool that provides insights and recommendations for improving loading times.
- Screaming Frog (https://www.screamingfrog.co.uk/seo-spider/): A website crawler that helps identify technical SEO issues, such as broken links, duplicate content, and missing meta tags.
- Google Search Console (https://search.google.com/search-console/): Provides insights into your website's performance, crawl errors, and indexing status.

Content Creation for SEO

Creating high-quality, relevant, and engaging content is essential for SEO. Content that provides value to users and addresses their needs is more likely to rank higher in search results. Key elements of content creation for SEO include:

1. Keyword Integration: Incorporate the target keyword naturally throughout the content, including in the title, headers, introduction, body, and conclusion. Avoid keyword stuffing, as it can harm your rankings and negatively impact user experience.
2. Content Length and Depth: Longer, in-depth content tends to perform better in search results. Aim to create comprehensive content that covers the topic thoroughly and provides valuable insights. However, prioritize quality over quantity, and ensure that the content remains engaging and easy to read.
3. Readability and Structure: Write content that is easy to read and understand. Use short paragraphs, bullet points, and subheadings to break up the text and improve readability. Use a conversational tone and avoid jargon or complex language.

4. **Visual Content:** Incorporate visual elements like images, infographics, videos, and charts to enhance the content and improve user engagement. Visual content can help illustrate key points, simplify complex topics, and make the content more appealing.
5. **Internal and External Links:** Include internal links to relevant pages on your website to improve navigation and guide users to additional content. Use external links to reputable sources to provide additional context and support your points.
6. **Regular Updates:** Regularly update your content to ensure that it remains accurate, relevant, and up-to-date. Search engines favor fresh content, and updating your articles can help maintain or improve their rankings.

Tools for Content Creation:

- Grammarly (https://www.grammarly.com/): A writing assistant that helps you produce clear, error-free, and engaging written content.
- Hemingway Editor (http://www.hemingwayapp.com/): A writing tool that improves readability by identifying complex sentences and suggesting simpler alternatives.
- Canva (https://www.canva.com/): A design tool for creating visually appealing graphics, infographics, and social media posts.
- BuzzSumo (https://buzzsumo.com/): Helps you identify popular content and trends within your industry, providing insights into what resonates with your audience.

Measuring SEO Performance

Measuring the performance of your SEO efforts is essential for understanding what's working, what's not, and how you can improve. By tracking key metrics and analyzing the data, you can make data-driven decisions and optimize your SEO strategy for better results. Key metrics to track include:

1. **Organic Traffic:** The number of visitors who arrive at your website through organic search results. Tools like Google Analytics (https://analytics.google.com/) provide detailed insights into your organic traffic, including the sources, user behavior, and conversion rates.

2. Keyword Rankings: The positions of your target keywords in search engine results pages (SERPs). Use tools like Ahrefs (https://ahrefs.com/), SEMrush (https://www.semrush.com/), and Moz (https://moz.com/) to track your keyword rankings and monitor changes over time.
3. Backlinks: The number and quality of backlinks pointing to your website. Tools like Ahrefs (https://ahrefs.com/), Moz Link Explorer (https://moz.com/link-explorer), and Majestic (https://majestic.com/) help you analyze your backlink profile and identify link-building opportunities.
4. Click-Through Rate (CTR): The percentage of users who click on your search engine listing when it appears in search results. Higher CTRs indicate that your title tags and meta descriptions are compelling and relevant. Use Google Search Console (https://search.google.com/search-console/) to monitor your CTR and identify opportunities for improvement.
5. Bounce Rate: The percentage of visitors who leave your website after viewing only one page. A high bounce rate may indicate that your content or user experience needs improvement. Use Google Analytics (https://analytics.google.com/) to track your bounce rate and identify pages with high exit rates.
6. Conversion Rate: The percentage of visitors who complete a desired action, such as making a purchase, filling out a form, or signing up for a newsletter. Conversion rate is a key indicator of the effectiveness of your SEO efforts in driving valuable actions. Use Google Analytics (https://analytics.google.com/) to track your conversion rates and set up goals.
7. Page Load Time: The time it takes for your web pages to load. Page load time is a critical ranking factor and directly impacts user experience. Use tools like Google PageSpeed Insights (https://developers.google.com/speed/pagespeed/insights/) and GTmetrix (https://gtmetrix.com/) to measure and optimize your page load times.

Tools for Measuring SEO Performance:

- Google Analytics (https://analytics.google.com/): Provides insights into website traffic, user behavior, and conversion rates.

- Google Search Console (https://search.google.com/search-console/): Offers data on your website's performance in search results, including keyword rankings, CTR, and crawl errors.
- Ahrefs (https://ahrefs.com/): A comprehensive SEO tool for tracking keyword rankings, backlinks, and organic traffic.
- SEMrush (https://www.semrush.com/): An all-in-one SEO tool for keyword research, competitor analysis, and performance tracking.
- Moz (https://moz.com/): Provides tools for keyword tracking, backlink analysis, and on-page optimization.
- GTmetrix (https://gtmetrix.com/): A website performance testing tool that provides insights and recommendations for improving loading times.

Real-World Examples of Successful SEO Strategies

Several companies have successfully leveraged SEO to achieve remarkable results. Here are a few notable examples:

1. HubSpot: HubSpot is a leader in inbound marketing and SEO. The company's blog covers a wide range of topics, including marketing, sales, and customer service. HubSpot focuses on creating high-quality, in-depth content that addresses the needs and pain points of its audience. The company also uses a strategic internal linking structure to improve site navigation and distribute link equity across its pages. HubSpot's commitment to SEO has helped it attract millions of organic visitors each month and establish itself as an authority in the marketing industry.
2. Moz: Moz, a provider of SEO software and tools, has built a reputation for producing valuable, educational content for the SEO and digital marketing community. Moz's blog covers a wide range of SEO topics, including keyword research, link building, and technical SEO. The company also offers resources like the Beginner's Guide to SEO and

Whiteboard Friday videos. Moz's focus on high-quality content and SEO best practices has helped it achieve high search rankings and drive significant organic traffic.
3. Backlinko: Backlinko, founded by Brian Dean, is known for its comprehensive and actionable SEO content. Brian Dean focuses on creating in-depth, high-quality guides and case studies that provide valuable insights and strategies for improving SEO. Backlinko's content is optimized for target keywords, includes internal and external links, and uses visual elements to enhance engagement. This approach has helped Backlinko rank for competitive keywords and attract a large audience of SEO professionals and marketers.
4. Airbnb: Airbnb uses SEO to attract travelers and property owners to its platform. The company optimizes its website for location-based keywords, such as "vacation rentals in Paris" or "apartments in New York." Airbnb also creates city-specific landing pages that provide valuable information about local attractions, neighborhoods, and travel tips. By focusing on local SEO and high-quality content, Airbnb has established itself as a leading platform for vacation rentals and travel experiences.
5. The Wirecutter: The Wirecutter, a product review site owned by The New York Times, leverages SEO to drive organic traffic to its in-depth product reviews and buying guides. The site focuses on creating high-quality, comprehensive reviews that address the needs and questions of consumers. The Wirecutter uses keyword research to identify relevant search terms and optimize its content for those keywords. The site's commitment to SEO and high-quality content has helped it achieve high search rankings and attract a large audience of consumers looking for reliable product recommendations.

Conclusion

Content optimization and SEO are essential components of a successful digital marketing strategy. By optimizing your content for search engines and users, you can increase visibility, drive organic traffic, and improve engagement. Key elements of content optimization and SEO include keyword research, on-page optimization, technical SEO, content creation, and performance measurement. Regularly review and refine your SEO strategy to stay ahead of trends, adapt to changes, and continuously improve your marketing efforts.

Chapter 10: Analytics and Performance Measurement

Introduction to Analytics and Performance Measurement

Analytics and performance measurement involve tracking, analyzing, and interpreting data to understand the effectiveness of your marketing efforts. By leveraging analytics tools and techniques, you can gain valuable insights into user behavior, campaign performance, and overall business impact. This data-driven approach enables you to make informed decisions, optimize your strategies, and achieve better results.

In this chapter, we will explore the key components of analytics and performance measurement, including setting goals and KPIs, using analytics tools, tracking key metrics, and interpreting data.

The Importance of Analytics and Performance Measurement

Analytics and performance measurement are crucial for several reasons:

1. Data-Driven Decisions: Analytics provides the data and insights needed to make informed decisions. By understanding what's working and what's not, you can optimize your strategies and allocate resources more effectively.
2. Performance Optimization: Tracking key metrics and analyzing data helps you identify areas for improvement and optimize your marketing efforts for better results. Continuous optimization leads to higher efficiency and effectiveness.
3. Accountability and Transparency: Analytics provides a clear and measurable way to evaluate the success of your marketing efforts. Accountability and transparency help build trust with stakeholders and demonstrate the value of your marketing investments.
4. Customer Insights: Analytics provides valuable insights into customer behavior, preferences, and pain points. Understanding your audience helps you create more targeted and relevant marketing campaigns.

5. ROI Measurement: Analytics enables you to measure the return on investment (ROI) of your marketing efforts. By comparing the revenue generated to the costs incurred, you can evaluate the financial effectiveness of your campaigns and make data-driven decisions.

Setting Goals and KPIs

Setting clear goals and key performance indicators (KPIs) is the foundation of effective analytics and performance measurement. Goals define what you want to achieve, while KPIs are the specific metrics used to measure progress toward those goals.

1. Define Your Goals: Clearly define the goals of your marketing efforts. Goals should be specific, measurable, achievable, relevant, and time-bound (SMART). Examples of marketing goals include increasing website traffic, generating leads, boosting sales, and improving brand awareness.
2. Identify KPIs: Identify the key performance indicators (KPIs) that align with your goals and provide a clear way to measure success. KPIs should be quantifiable and directly related to your goals. Examples of KPIs include website traffic, conversion rate, cost per acquisition (CPA), return on ad spend (ROAS), and customer lifetime value (CLV).
3. Set Benchmarks and Targets: Establish benchmarks and targets for your KPIs based on historical data, industry standards, and your specific goals. Benchmarks provide a point of reference for evaluating performance, while targets define the desired outcome.

Examples of Goals and KPIs:

- Goal: Increase website traffic by 20% in the next six months.
    - KPIs: Organic traffic, referral traffic, direct traffic, social media traffic.
- Goal: Generate 500 new leads per month.
    - KPIs: Number of leads, conversion rate, cost per lead (CPL).
- Goal: Boost online sales by 15% in Q4.
    - KPIs: Sales revenue, number of transactions, average order value (AOV), conversion rate.
- Goal: Improve email open rates by 10% in the next three months.
    - KPIs: Open rate, click-through rate (CTR), unsubscribe rate, email engagement.

Using Analytics Tools

Analytics tools provide the data and insights needed to track and measure the performance of your marketing efforts. These tools offer a wide range of features, including data collection, reporting, visualization, and analysis.

1. Google Analytics: Google Analytics (https://analytics.google.com/) is a powerful and widely used web analytics tool that provides insights into website traffic, user behavior, and conversion metrics. Key features include real-time reporting, audience analysis, acquisition channels, behavior flow, and goal tracking.
2. Google Search Console: Google Search Console (https://search.google.com/search-console/) provides data on your website's performance in search results, including keyword rankings, CTR, and crawl errors. It also offers tools for submitting sitemaps, monitoring backlinks, and identifying technical SEO issues.
3. SEMrush: SEMrush (https://www.semrush.com/) is an all-in-one marketing tool that offers features for SEO, PPC, content marketing, and competitive analysis. Key features include keyword research, site audits, backlink analysis, and performance tracking.
4. Ahrefs: Ahrefs (https://ahrefs.com/) is an SEO tool that provides insights into keyword rankings, backlinks, and organic traffic. Key features include keyword research, site audits, content analysis, and competitor analysis.
5. HubSpot: HubSpot (https://www.hubspot.com/) is an all-in-one marketing, sales, and customer service platform that offers tools for lead generation, email marketing, social media management, and analytics. Key features include CRM integration, marketing automation, and performance tracking.
6. Google Data Studio: Google Data Studio (https://datastudio.google.com/) is a data visualization and reporting tool that allows you to create interactive and customizable dashboards. You can connect Data Studio to various data sources, including Google Analytics, Google Ads, and Google Sheets.

Tools for Analytics and Performance Measurement:

- Google Analytics (https://analytics.google.com/): Provides insights into website traffic, user behavior, and conversion metrics.

- Google Search Console (https://search.google.com/search-console/): Offers data on your website's performance in search results, including keyword rankings and crawl errors.
- SEMrush (https://www.semrush.com/): An all-in-one marketing tool for keyword research, competitor analysis, and performance tracking.
- Ahrefs (https://ahrefs.com/): An SEO tool for tracking keyword rankings, backlinks, and organic traffic.
- HubSpot (https://www.hubspot.com/): An all-in-one marketing, sales, and customer service platform with performance tracking features.
- Google Data Studio (https://datastudio.google.com/): A data visualization and reporting tool for creating interactive and customizable dashboards.

Tracking Key Metrics

Tracking key metrics is essential for understanding the performance of your marketing efforts and identifying areas for improvement. Here are some important metrics to track across various channels:

1. Website Metrics:
    - Sessions: The number of visits to your website.
    - Users: The number of unique visitors to your website.
    - Pageviews: The total number of pages viewed on your website.
    - Average Session Duration: The average amount of time users spend on your website.
    - Bounce Rate: The percentage of visitors who leave your website after viewing only one page.
    - Conversion Rate: The percentage of visitors who complete a desired action, such as making a purchase or filling out a form.
2. SEO Metrics:
    - Organic Traffic: The number of visitors who arrive at your website through organic search results.

- Keyword Rankings: The positions of your target keywords in search engine results pages (SERPs).
- Backlinks: The number and quality of backlinks pointing to your website.
- Click-Through Rate (CTR): The percentage of users who click on your search engine listing when it appears in search results.
- Domain Authority (DA): A metric that predicts how well a website will rank on search engines.

3. PPC Metrics:
    - Impressions: The number of times your ad is displayed.
    - Clicks: The number of times users click on your ad.
    - Click-Through Rate (CTR): The percentage of clicks your ad receives relative to the number of impressions.
    - Cost Per Click (CPC): The average amount you pay for each click on your ad.
    - Conversion Rate: The percentage of users who complete a desired action after clicking on your ad.
    - Return on Ad Spend (ROAS): The revenue generated for every dollar spent on advertising.

4. Email Marketing Metrics:
    - Open Rate: The percentage of recipients who open your email.
    - Click-Through Rate (CTR): The percentage of recipients who click on a link within your email.
    - Conversion Rate: The percentage of recipients who complete a desired action after clicking on a link within your email.
    - Bounce Rate: The percentage of emails that are not delivered successfully to recipients' inboxes.
    - Unsubscribe Rate: The percentage of recipients who unsubscribe from your email list.

5. Social Media Metrics:
    - Reach: The total number of unique users who see your content.
    - Engagement: The number of likes, comments, shares, and overall interaction with your content.

- Click-Through Rate (CTR): The percentage of users who click on a link within your social media post.
- Follower Growth: The increase in the number of followers over a specific period.
- Conversions: The number of desired actions completed by users, such as making a purchase or signing up for a newsletter.

Interpreting Data

Interpreting data involves analyzing the metrics you've tracked to gain insights and make informed decisions. Here are some steps to help you interpret your data effectively:

1. Compare Against Benchmarks: Compare your metrics against industry benchmarks, historical data, and your set targets. This will help you understand how your performance stacks up and identify areas for improvement.
2. Identify Trends and Patterns: Look for trends and patterns in your data over time. For example, identify periods of increased traffic, spikes in engagement, or changes in conversion rates. Understanding these patterns can help you identify the factors driving performance and inform your strategy.
3. Segment Your Data: Break down your data into segments to gain deeper insights. For example, analyze traffic sources, user demographics, device types, and geographic locations. Segmenting your data helps you understand how different audience groups interact with your content and what drives their behavior.
4. Analyze User Behavior: Use tools like Google Analytics to analyze user behavior on your website. Look at metrics such as user flow, time on site, and pages per session to understand how visitors navigate your site and where they drop off. This information can help you optimize your website's structure and content.
5. Evaluate Campaign Effectiveness: Assess the effectiveness of your marketing campaigns by comparing the results against your goals and KPIs. Identify which campaigns performed well and which ones fell short. Use these insights to refine your campaigns and improve future performance.

6. Use Data Visualization: Create visual representations of your data, such as charts, graphs, and dashboards. Data visualization helps you identify trends, patterns, and outliers more easily and communicate your findings to stakeholders.

Conclusion

Analytics and performance measurement are essential components of a successful marketing strategy. By setting clear goals and KPIs, using analytics tools, tracking key metrics, and interpreting data, you can gain valuable insights into the effectiveness of your marketing efforts and make data-driven decisions. Regularly review and refine your analytics strategy to stay ahead of trends, adapt to changes, and continuously improve your marketing performance.

Chapter 11: Integrated Marketing Strategies

Introduction to Integrated Marketing Strategies

Integrated marketing strategies involve coordinating and aligning all marketing channels and tactics to deliver a consistent and cohesive message to your audience. By integrating various marketing efforts, you can create a seamless customer experience, reinforce your brand message, and achieve better results.

In this chapter, we will explore the key components of integrated marketing strategies, including the benefits, planning process, execution, and measurement.

The Importance of Integrated Marketing Strategies

Integrated marketing strategies are crucial for several reasons:

1. Consistency: Integrated marketing ensures that all marketing channels and tactics deliver a consistent message and brand experience. Consistency helps reinforce your brand identity and build trust with your audience.
2. Synergy: By coordinating various marketing efforts, you can create synergy and amplify the impact of your campaigns. Integrated marketing leverages the strengths of different channels to achieve a greater overall effect.
3. Efficiency: Integrated marketing strategies streamline your marketing efforts and eliminate duplication and inefficiencies. By aligning your tactics, you can optimize resource allocation and achieve better results with less effort.
4. Improved Customer Experience: Integrated marketing creates a seamless and cohesive customer experience across all touchpoints. A consistent and positive experience enhances customer satisfaction and loyalty.
5. Data-Driven Insights: Integrated marketing strategies provide a holistic view of your marketing performance. By analyzing data from various channels, you can gain deeper insights into customer behavior and preferences and make more informed decisions.

Planning an Integrated Marketing Strategy

Planning an integrated marketing strategy involves several key steps:

1. Define Your Goals: Clearly define the goals of your integrated marketing strategy. Your goals should be specific, measurable, achievable, relevant, and time-bound (SMART). Examples of goals include increasing brand awareness, generating leads, boosting sales, and improving customer retention.
2. Identify Your Target Audience: Conduct audience research to understand your target audience's demographics, interests, behaviors, and pain points. Create buyer personas to represent different segments of your audience and tailor your marketing efforts to meet their needs.
3. Develop Your Brand Message: Define your brand message and value proposition. Your brand message should be clear, consistent, and resonate with your target audience. Ensure that all marketing channels and tactics deliver this message cohesively.
4. Select Marketing Channels: Choose the marketing channels that align with your goals and audience preferences. Consider a mix of online and offline channels, such as content marketing, social media, email marketing, PPC advertising, SEO, events, and direct mail.
5. Create a Content Plan: Develop a content plan that outlines the types of content you will produce, the topics you will cover, and the publishing schedule. Your content should align with your brand message and provide value to your audience.
6. Coordinate Marketing Efforts: Ensure that all marketing channels and tactics are coordinated and aligned with your overall strategy. Create a detailed marketing calendar that outlines the timing and execution of each campaign. Use project management tools to collaborate and track progress.

Executing an Integrated Marketing Strategy

Executing an integrated marketing strategy involves coordinating and implementing your marketing efforts across various channels. Follow these steps to ensure successful execution:

1. Consistent Branding: Maintain consistent branding across all marketing channels, including visual elements (e.g., logo, color scheme), tone of voice, and messaging. Consistency reinforces your brand identity and creates a cohesive experience for your audience.
2. Cross-Channel Promotion: Promote your content and campaigns across multiple channels to maximize reach and engagement. For example, share blog posts on social media, include links to landing pages in email newsletters, and use PPC ads to drive traffic to your website.
3. Unified Customer Experience: Create a seamless and integrated customer experience across all touchpoints. Ensure that your website, social media profiles, email communications, and offline interactions provide a consistent and positive experience.
4. Leverage Data and Analytics: Use data and analytics to monitor the performance of your integrated marketing efforts. Track key metrics, such as website traffic, engagement, conversions, and ROI, to evaluate the effectiveness of your campaigns. Use these insights to optimize your strategy and make data-driven decisions.
5. Collaborate and Communicate: Foster collaboration and communication among your marketing team and other departments. Regularly share updates, insights, and feedback to ensure alignment and coordination. Use project management and collaboration tools to streamline communication and track progress.

Measuring the Success of Integrated Marketing Strategies

Measuring the success of integrated marketing strategies involves tracking key metrics and analyzing data from various channels. Follow these steps to evaluate the performance of your integrated marketing efforts:

1. Track Key Metrics: Identify and track key performance indicators (KPIs) that align with your integrated marketing goals. These metrics will help you gauge the effectiveness of your strategy. Examples include:
- Brand Awareness: Social media reach, impressions, website traffic, and brand mentions.
- Engagement: Likes, comments, shares, click-through rates (CTR), and time spent on site.
- Lead Generation: Number of leads, conversion rates, cost per lead (CPL), and lead quality.
- Sales and Revenue: Sales volume, sales conversion rates, customer acquisition cost (CAC), and return on investment (ROI).
- Customer Retention: Customer satisfaction scores, retention rates, repeat purchase rates, and customer lifetime value (CLV).
2. Use Integrated Analytics Tools: Utilize tools that provide a comprehensive view of your marketing performance across all channels. These tools help you consolidate data, visualize trends, and generate insights.
    - Google Analytics (https://analytics.google.com/): Tracks website performance, user behavior, and conversion metrics.
    - HubSpot (https://www.hubspot.com/): An all-in-one marketing platform that offers CRM integration, marketing automation, and performance tracking.
    - Hootsuite (https://hootsuite.com/): A social media management tool that provides analytics and reporting features to track social media performance.
    - Google Data Studio (https://datastudio.google.com/): A data visualization tool for creating interactive and customizable dashboards.
    - Tableau (https://www.tableau.com/): A powerful data visualization tool for creating comprehensive reports and dashboards.
3. Analyze Data and Identify Insights: Regularly review your analytics data to identify trends, patterns, and insights. Look for correlations between different metrics and channels to understand how they influence each other. Use these insights to identify areas for improvement and optimize your integrated marketing strategy.
4. Report and Communicate Results: Create regular reports to communicate your integrated marketing performance to stakeholders. Use data visualization tools to present your

findings in a clear and compelling way. Highlight key achievements, areas for improvement, and actionable recommendations.
5. Refine and Optimize: Based on your analysis and insights, continuously refine and optimize your integrated marketing strategy. Experiment with different tactics, channels, and content to find what works best for your audience. Regularly update your strategy to stay ahead of trends and adapt to changes in the market.

Real-World Examples of Successful Integrated Marketing Strategies

Several companies have successfully executed integrated marketing strategies to achieve remarkable results. Here are a few notable examples:

1. Coca-Cola: Coca-Cola's "Share a Coke" campaign is a classic example of integrated marketing. The campaign involved personalized Coke bottles with popular names and encouraged consumers to share photos on social media using the hashtag #ShareaCoke. Coca-Cola integrated various channels, including social media, print, TV ads, and in-store promotions, to create a cohesive and engaging campaign. The result was a significant increase in brand engagement and sales.
2. Nike: Nike's "Just Do It" campaign is another excellent example of integrated marketing. The campaign featured inspirational stories of athletes overcoming challenges and achieving greatness. Nike used a mix of TV ads, social media, influencer partnerships, and experiential marketing to deliver a consistent and powerful message. The campaign reinforced Nike's brand identity and resonated with a wide audience, driving brand loyalty and sales.
3. Apple: Apple's product launches are masterclasses in integrated marketing. The company creates anticipation and excitement through carefully coordinated efforts across multiple channels. Apple uses teaser videos, social media, email marketing, press releases, and live events to build buzz and attract attention. Consistent and cohesive messaging ensures a seamless experience for customers and reinforces Apple's brand image.
4. Starbucks: Starbucks' "Red Cup" campaign is a successful example of seasonal integrated marketing. Each year, Starbucks launches its holiday-themed red cups and

promotes them through social media, in-store displays, email newsletters, and special promotions. The campaign creates a sense of tradition and excitement, driving customer engagement and sales during the holiday season.

Conclusion

Integrated marketing strategies are essential for delivering a consistent and cohesive message to your audience, creating synergy across channels, and achieving better results. By planning, executing, and measuring your integrated marketing efforts, you can create a seamless customer experience, reinforce your brand message, and optimize your marketing performance. Regularly review and refine your integrated marketing strategy to stay ahead of trends, adapt to changes, and continuously improve your marketing efforts.

Chapter 12: Future Trends in Digital Marketing

Introduction to Future Trends in Digital Marketing

The digital marketing landscape is constantly evolving, driven by technological advancements, changing consumer behaviors, and emerging trends. Staying ahead of these trends is crucial for businesses to remain competitive and effectively engage with their audience. In this chapter, we will explore some of the key future trends in digital marketing and provide insights on how businesses can adapt and thrive.

Key Future Trends in Digital Marketing

1. Artificial Intelligence (AI) and Machine Learning: AI and machine learning are transforming digital marketing by enabling more personalized and data-driven marketing strategies. AI-powered tools can analyze vast amounts of data, predict consumer behavior, and automate tasks such as content creation, ad targeting, and customer segmentation. Businesses can leverage AI to enhance customer experiences, optimize campaigns, and improve decision-making.

2. Voice Search Optimization: With the increasing popularity of voice-activated devices like Amazon Alexa, Google Home, and Apple's Siri, voice search is becoming a significant trend in digital marketing. Businesses need to optimize their content for voice search by focusing on natural language, long-tail keywords, and conversational queries. Voice search optimization can improve visibility and drive traffic from voice-activated devices.

3. Video Marketing: Video continues to be a dominant content format, driving engagement and conversions. Live streaming, short-form videos (e.g., TikTok, Instagram Reels), and interactive videos are gaining popularity. Businesses should invest in video marketing by creating high-quality, engaging, and shareable video content that resonates with their audience.

4. Augmented Reality (AR) and Virtual Reality (VR): AR and VR technologies are revolutionizing the way consumers interact with brands. AR and VR provide immersive

and interactive experiences, allowing customers to visualize products, explore virtual environments, and engage with branded content. Businesses can leverage AR and VR to enhance customer experiences, drive engagement, and differentiate themselves from competitors.

5. Influencer Marketing Evolution: Influencer marketing is evolving, with a focus on authenticity, micro-influencers, and long-term partnerships. Consumers are becoming more discerning, and they value genuine and relatable content. Businesses should prioritize building authentic relationships with influencers, collaborating with micro-influencers who have niche audiences, and fostering long-term partnerships to drive meaningful engagement.

6. Personalization and Hyper-Targeting: Personalization is becoming increasingly important in digital marketing. Consumers expect tailored experiences and relevant content. Businesses can leverage data and AI to deliver personalized messages, offers, and recommendations based on individual preferences, behaviors, and demographics. Hyper-targeting allows businesses to reach specific audience segments with precision and relevance.

7. Privacy and Data Protection: With growing concerns about data privacy and regulatory changes (e.g., GDPR, CCPA), businesses need to prioritize data protection and transparency. Consumers are becoming more aware of how their data is used, and they value brands that respect their privacy. Businesses should implement robust data protection measures, be transparent about data practices, and build trust with their audience.

8. Sustainability and Social Responsibility: Consumers are increasingly conscious of sustainability and social responsibility. Brands that demonstrate a commitment to ethical practices, environmental sustainability, and social causes can build stronger connections with their audience. Businesses should incorporate sustainability and social responsibility into their marketing strategies and communicate their efforts authentically.

Adapting to Future Trends

To stay ahead of future trends in digital marketing, businesses should:

1. Stay Informed: Keep up-to-date with the latest trends, technologies, and best practices in digital marketing. Follow industry blogs, attend webinars and conferences, and participate in online communities to stay informed.
2. Experiment and Innovate: Be open to experimenting with new technologies and marketing strategies. Test different approaches, measure results, and iterate based on data and insights. Innovation is key to staying competitive and meeting evolving consumer expectations.
3. Invest in Technology: Invest in the right technologies and tools to enhance your digital marketing efforts. AI, automation, data analytics, and content creation tools can help you optimize campaigns, personalize experiences, and improve efficiency.
4. Focus on Customer Experience: Prioritize delivering exceptional customer experiences across all touchpoints. Understand your audience's needs, preferences, and pain points, and tailor your marketing efforts to provide value and address their concerns.
5. Build Authentic Relationships: Foster authentic relationships with your audience, influencers, and partners. Authenticity builds trust and loyalty, and it resonates with consumers who value genuine connections.
6. Embrace Sustainability: Incorporate sustainability and social responsibility into your marketing strategy. Communicate your efforts transparently and authentically, and demonstrate your commitment to ethical practices and social causes.

Conclusion

The future of digital marketing is dynamic and ever evolving, driven by technological advancements, changing consumer behaviours, and emerging trends. By staying informed, experimenting with new approaches, investing in technology, focusing on customer experience, building authentic relationships, and embracing sustainability, businesses can adapt and thrive in the digital landscape. Regularly review and refine your digital marketing strategy to stay ahead of trends, adapt to changes, and continuously improve your marketing efforts.

Chapter 13: Case Studies and Success Stories

Introduction to Case Studies and Success Stories

Case studies and success stories provide real-world examples of how businesses have successfully implemented digital marketing strategies to achieve their goals. Analyzing these examples can offer valuable insights, inspire new ideas, and highlight best practices that you can apply to your own marketing efforts.

Case Study 1: Airbnb's Content Marketing and SEO Strategy

Background: Airbnb is a global online marketplace for lodging and travel experiences. The company wanted to increase organic traffic and improve its search engine rankings.

Strategy: Airbnb implemented a comprehensive content marketing and SEO strategy, focusing on creating high-quality, location-specific content. Key elements of their strategy included:

1. City Guides: Airbnb created detailed city guides that provided valuable information about local attractions, neighborhoods, and travel tips. These guides were optimized for relevant keywords and included high-quality images and user-generated content.
2. User-Generated Content: Airbnb encouraged users to share their travel experiences and reviews on the platform. This user-generated content added authenticity and provided valuable insights for other travelers.
3. Local SEO: Airbnb optimized its website for local search by targeting location-based keywords, creating city-specific landing pages, and ensuring that the content was relevant and valuable to users.

Results: Airbnb's content marketing and SEO strategy led to a significant increase in organic traffic and higher search engine rankings. The company successfully positioned itself as a trusted source of travel information and experiences.

Case Study 2: Coca-Cola's "Share a Coke" Campaign

Background: Coca-Cola launched the "Share a Coke" campaign to increase brand engagement and drive sales. The campaign involved personalizing Coke bottles with popular names and encouraging consumers to share their experiences on social media.

Strategy: Coca-Cola implemented an integrated marketing strategy that included:

1. Personalized Products: Coca-Cola printed popular names on Coke bottles and cans, making the product more personal and shareable.
2. Social Media Engagement: The company encouraged consumers to share photos of their personalized Coke bottles using the hashtag #ShareaCoke. Coca-Cola featured user-generated content on its social media profiles and website.
3. In-Store Promotions: Coca-Cola used in-store displays and promotions to highlight the personalized products and encourage purchases.
4. Traditional Advertising: The campaign was supported by TV commercials, print ads, and outdoor advertising, all promoting the "Share a Coke" message.

Results: The "Share a Coke" campaign was a massive success, leading to a significant increase in brand engagement, social media mentions, and sales. The campaign strengthened Coca-Cola's brand image and created a sense of community among consumers.

Case Study 3: HubSpot's Inbound Marketing Strategy

Background: HubSpot is a provider of inbound marketing and sales software. The company wanted to attract and convert more leads through its website.

Strategy: HubSpot implemented an inbound marketing strategy focused on attracting, engaging, and delighting customers. Key elements of their strategy included:

1. Content Creation: HubSpot created high-quality, educational content, including blog posts, ebooks, webinars, and videos. The content addressed the pain points and needs of their target audience.
2. SEO Optimization: HubSpot optimized its content for relevant keywords to improve search engine rankings and attract organic traffic.
3. Lead Capture: The company used lead magnets, such as ebooks and webinars, to capture email addresses and generate leads. Visitors could access valuable content in exchange for their contact information.
4. Marketing Automation: HubSpot used marketing automation to nurture leads through personalized email campaigns and workflows. The automation tools helped segment leads, deliver relevant content, and guide them through the sales funnel.
5. Social Media Marketing: HubSpot promoted its content on social media to reach a wider audience and drive traffic to its website.

Results: HubSpot's inbound marketing strategy led to a significant increase in website traffic, lead generation, and customer conversions. The company successfully positioned itself as a thought leader in the marketing industry and built a loyal customer base.

Case Study 4: Nike's "Just Do It" Campaign

Background: Nike's "Just Do It" campaign aimed to inspire and motivate people to pursue their athletic goals. The campaign emphasized the brand's core values of determination, empowerment, and achievement.

Strategy: Nike implemented an integrated marketing strategy that included:

1. Inspirational Content: Nike created powerful and emotional content that featured athletes overcoming challenges and achieving greatness. The content was shared through TV commercials, social media, and digital platforms.
2. Influencer Partnerships: Nike collaborated with high-profile athletes and influencers to amplify the campaign's message. These partnerships helped reach a wider audience and build credibility.

3. Social Media Engagement: Nike encouraged users to share their own stories and achievements using the hashtag #JustDoIt. The company featured user-generated content on its social media profiles and website.
4. Experiential Marketing: Nike organized events and activations that allowed consumers to engage with the brand and participate in athletic challenges.

Results: The "Just Do It" campaign resonated with a global audience and became one of the most iconic marketing campaigns in history. Nike successfully reinforced its brand identity, increased engagement, and drove sales.

Conclusion

Case studies and success stories provide valuable insights into how businesses have successfully implemented digital marketing strategies to achieve their goals. By analyzing these examples, you can gain inspiration, learn best practices, and apply similar tactics to your own marketing efforts. Remember that each business is unique, and it's essential to tailor your strategies to your specific goals, audience, and industry.

Chapter 14: Digital Marketing Tools and Resources

Introduction to Digital Marketing Tools and Resources

Digital marketing is enhanced by a myriad of tools and resources designed to streamline efforts, provide insights, and optimize campaigns. In this chapter, we will explore essential tools and resources across various aspects of digital marketing, including content creation, SEO, social media management, email marketing, analytics, and more.

Content Creation Tools

Creating high-quality content is crucial for engaging your audience and driving traffic. Here are some essential content creation tools:

1. Canva (https://www.canva.com/): A user-friendly design tool for creating graphics, infographics, social media posts, and more. Canva offers a wide range of templates and customization options.
2. Grammarly (https://www.grammarly.com/): An AI-powered writing assistant that helps you produce clear, error-free, and engaging written content. Grammarly provides grammar and style suggestions, plagiarism checks, and more.
3. Hemingway Editor (http://www.hemingwayapp.com/): A writing tool that improves readability by identifying complex sentences and suggesting simpler alternatives. It highlights adverbs, passive voice, and difficult-to-read sentences.
4. Adobe Creative Cloud (https://www.adobe.com/creativecloud.html): A suite of professional design and editing tools, including Photoshop, Illustrator, and Premiere Pro. Ideal for creating high-quality visuals and videos.
5. BuzzSumo (https://buzzsumo.com/): A content research tool that helps you identify popular content and trends within your industry. BuzzSumo provides insights into what resonates with your audience.

SEO Tools

SEO tools help you optimize your website to rank higher in search engine results and attract organic traffic. Here are some essential SEO tools:

1. Google Keyword Planner (https://ads.google.com/home/tools/keyword-planner/): Provides keyword ideas, search volume, and competition data. Useful for keyword research and planning.
2. Ahrefs (https://ahrefs.com/): A comprehensive SEO tool for keyword research, competitor analysis, backlink analysis, and performance tracking.
3. SEMrush (https://www.semrush.com/): An all-in-one SEO tool for keyword research, competitor analysis, site audit, and performance tracking.
4. Moz (https://moz.com/): Provides tools for keyword tracking, backlink analysis, and on-page optimization. Moz also offers educational resources and community support.
5. Screaming Frog SEO Spider (https://www.screamingfrog.co.uk/seo-spider/): A website crawler that helps identify on-page SEO issues, such as broken links, duplicate content, and missing meta tags.

Social Media Management Tools

Social media management tools help you schedule posts, track performance, and engage with your audience. Here are some essential social media management tools:

1. Hootsuite (https://hootsuite.com/): A social media management platform that allows you to schedule posts, track performance, and manage multiple social media accounts.
2. Buffer (https://buffer.com/): A social media scheduling tool that helps you plan and publish content across multiple social media platforms. Buffer also offers analytics and engagement features.
3. Sprout Social (https://sproutsocial.com/): A comprehensive social media management tool that offers scheduling, analytics, and engagement features. Sprout Social also provides social listening and reporting tools.
4. Later (https://later.com/): A visual social media scheduler for Instagram, Facebook, Twitter, and Pinterest. Later offers a drag-and-drop calendar and visual planning features.

5. SocialBee (https://socialbee.io/): A social media management tool that helps you schedule posts, curate content, and grow your social media presence.

Email Marketing Tools

Email marketing tools help you create, send, and track email campaigns. Here are some essential email marketing tools:

1. Mailchimp (https://mailchimp.com/): An email marketing platform that offers tools for creating, sending, and analyzing email campaigns. Mailchimp also provides marketing automation and CRM features.
2. ConvertKit (https://convertkit.com/): An email marketing tool designed for creators and bloggers. ConvertKit offers features for email design, automation, and personalization.
3. ActiveCampaign (https://www.activecampaign.com/): An email marketing and automation platform that helps you create personalized email campaigns and workflows.
4. Sendinblue (https://www.sendinblue.com/): An email marketing platform that offers email design, automation, and performance tracking features. Sendinblue also provides SMS marketing and CRM tools.
5. MailerLite (https://www.mailerlite.com/): An email marketing tool that offers drag-and-drop email design, automation, and analytics features. MailerLite is known for its simplicity and ease of use.

Analytics and Performance Measurement Tools

Analytics tools help you track and measure the performance of your marketing efforts. Here are some essential analytics tools:

1. Google Analytics (https://analytics.google.com/): A powerful web analytics tool that provides insights into website traffic, user behavior, and conversion metrics. Google Analytics offers real-time reporting, audience analysis, and goal tracking features.

2. Google Search Console (https://search.google.com/search-console/): Provides data on your website's performance in search results, including keyword rankings, CTR, and crawl errors. It also offers tools for submitting sitemaps and monitoring backlinks.
3. Google Data Studio (https://datastudio.google.com/): A data visualization and reporting tool that allows you to create interactive and customizable dashboards. You can connect Data Studio to various data sources, including Google Analytics, Google Ads, and Google Sheets.
4. SEMrush (https://www.semrush.com/): An all-in-one marketing tool that offers performance tracking, keyword research, and competitor analysis features.
5. Tableau (https://www.tableau.com/): A powerful data visualization tool for creating comprehensive reports and dashboards. Tableau helps you analyze and interpret complex data.

Additional Resources

Investing in continuous learning and staying updated with the latest industry trends is crucial for digital marketing success. Here are some additional resources to help you stay informed and enhance your skills:

1. Blogs and Websites:
    - Moz Blog (https://moz.com/blog): Offers insights, tips, and best practices on SEO and digital marketing.
    - HubSpot Blog (https://blog.hubspot.com/): Covers a wide range of topics, including inbound marketing, SEO, social media, and sales.
    - Neil Patel Blog (https://neilpatel.com/blog/): Provides actionable advice on SEO, content marketing, and digital marketing strategies.
    - Content Marketing Institute (https://contentmarketinginstitute.com/blog/): Offers resources and insights on content marketing best practices and trends.
2. Online Courses and Certifications:
    - Google Analytics Academy (https://analytics.google.com/analytics/academy/): Free courses on Google Analytics and data analysis.

- HubSpot Academy (https://academy.hubspot.com/): Free courses and certifications on inbound marketing, content marketing, email marketing, and more.
- Coursera (https://www.coursera.org/): Offers online courses on various digital marketing topics, including SEO, social media marketing, and data analytics.
- Udemy (https://www.udemy.com/): Provides a wide range of digital marketing courses, from beginner to advanced levels.

3. Books:
    - "Influence: The Psychology of Persuasion" by Robert B. Cialdini: Explores the psychology behind why people say "yes" and how to apply these principles in marketing.
    - "Contagious: How to Build Word of Mouth in the Digital Age" by Jonah Berger: Discusses why certain content goes viral and how to create contagious content.
    - "Made to Stick: Why Some Ideas Survive and Others Die" by Chip Heath and Dan Heath: Explores the principles of creating memorable and impactful messages.
    - "SEO 2024: Learn Search Engine Optimization with Smart Internet Marketing Strategies" by Adam Clarke: Provides updated SEO strategies and best practices.

4. Webinars and Conferences:
    - MozCon (https://moz.com/mozcon): An annual conference on SEO and digital marketing, featuring industry experts and thought leaders.
    - Content Marketing World (https://www.contentmarketingworld.com/): A conference focused on content marketing strategies and trends.
    - Inbound (https://www.inbound.com/): An annual event hosted by HubSpot, covering topics on inbound marketing, sales, and customer experience.
    - Social Media Marketing World (https://www.socialmediaexaminer.com/smmworld/): A conference dedicated to social media marketing strategies and best practices.

Conclusion

Digital marketing tools and resources are essential for optimizing your marketing efforts, gaining insights, and staying ahead of industry trends. By leveraging the right tools and continuously investing in learning and development, you can enhance your digital marketing strategy and achieve your business goals. Stay curious, be proactive, and embrace the ever-evolving landscape of digital marketing.

Final Thoughts

Digital marketing is a dynamic and ever-evolving field that requires continuous learning, experimentation, and adaptation. By leveraging the insights and strategies outlined in this guide, you can navigate the complexities of digital marketing and achieve your business goals.

Key takeaways include:

- Developing a Comprehensive Strategy: Start with a clear understanding of your goals, target audience, and competitive landscape. Develop a comprehensive digital marketing strategy that integrates various channels and tactics to deliver a consistent and cohesive message.
- Creating High-Quality Content: Content is the cornerstone of digital marketing. Focus on creating valuable, relevant, and engaging content that resonates with your audience and addresses their needs.
- Leveraging Data and Analytics: Use data and analytics to track performance, gain insights, and make data-driven decisions. Continuously optimize your strategies based on data and emerging trends.
- Embracing Innovation: Stay informed about the latest trends and technologies in digital marketing. Be open to experimenting with new approaches and innovating to stay competitive.

- Building Authentic Relationships: Foster authentic relationships with your audience, influencers, and partners. Authenticity builds trust and loyalty and resonates with consumers who value genuine connections.
- Focusing on Customer Experience: Prioritize delivering exceptional customer experiences across all touchpoints. Understand your audience's needs, preferences, and pain points, and tailor your marketing efforts to provide value and address their concerns.

By following these principles and continuously evolving your digital marketing strategies, you can achieve sustained success and drive meaningful results for your business.

www.ingramcontent.com/pod-product-compliance
Lightning Source LLC
Chambersburg PA
CBHW071939210526
45479CB00002B/743